What's the Problem?

What's the Problem?
A Brief Guide to Thinking Critically

Paula S. Rothenberg

Senior Fellow, Murphy Institute, City University of New York

WORTH PUBLISHERS

Senior Publisher: Catherine Woods
Acquisitions Editor: Erik Gilg
Marketing Manager: Amy Shefferd
Art Director: Babs Reingold
Text and Cover Designer: Kevin Kall
Associate Managing Editor: Tracey Kuehn
Project Editor: Dana Kasowitz
Production Manager: Barbara Anne Seixas
Composition: Northeastern Graphic, Inc.
Printing and Binding: RR Donnelley

Library of Congress Control Number: 2010924554

ISBN-13: 978-1-4292-4218-9
ISBN-10: 1-4292-4218-3

Printed in the United States of America

First printing 2010

Worth Publishers
41 Madison Avenue
New York, NY 10010
www.worthpublishers.com

Paula Rothenberg writes, lectures, and consults on a variety of topics, including multicultural curriculum transformation, issues of inequality, equity, and privilege, globalizing the curriculum, and white privilege. From 1989 to 2006, she served as Director of The New Jersey Project on Inclusive Scholarship, Curriculum, and Teaching, and Professor of Philosophy and Women's Studies at The William Paterson University of New Jersey. She is the author of *Invisible Privilege: A Memoir about Race, Class and Gender* (University Press of Kansas), and, with Worth Publishers, *Race, Class, and Gender,* Eighth Edition (2010) and *Beyond Borders: Thinking Critically about Global Issues* (2006); her anthology, *White Privilege: Readings on the Other Side of Racism,* will soon go into its fourth edition. Paula Rothenberg is also co-editor of a number of other anthologies, including *Creating an Inclusive College Curriculum: A Teaching Sourcebook from the New Jersey Project* and *Feminist Frameworks: Alternative Theoretical Accounts of the Relations between Women and Men.* Her articles and essays appear in journals and anthologies across the disciplines and many have been widely reprinted.

CONTENTS

8 It's the Solution, Not the Problem   132

Conclusion: What's the Problem? Questions and Answers   150

What's The Problem?

Thinking is a tricky business. Learning to think *critically* is even trickier. That's because critical thinking is as much about getting the *questions* right as it is about coming up with the right answers. If the problem is predicated on the wrong question or adopts the wrong conceptual framework, trying to answer it will lead you down the wrong path, possibly depositing you at a dead end or, even worse, getting you stuck in the mud.

This book is designed to help you learn to think critically by placing your focus on how questions or problems are posed and making you aware that much of the answer is already contained in the way the topic is formulated. This is because implicit in each topic or question is a particular way of seeing the world. Sometimes the view or perspective from which the problem arises is obvious and other times it is less so. But everything we think about comes to us from a particular perspective. Learning to identify the perspective is the first step toward thinking critically. It allows you to evaluate the assumptions that come with the perspective and to decide whether you want to buy into this way of seeing the world. It empowers you as a thinker to evaluate the worldview from which the problem or issue arises so that you that you can decide whether or not it is defensible. If it is, you can feel comfortable with proceeding, but if it is not, you'll know that it's best to start over.

For those of us who are concerned with working to create a more just and equitable world, it is important to understand whether the choices we make and the policies we support bring us closer to our goal. That's where critical thinking comes in. Learning to identify the hidden assumptions and unexamined values implicit in the way we frame our questions as well as our answers is an important step in that direction.

This book adopts what is known as an intersections approach, an approach that uses the lenses of race, class, and gender to make sense of the world. Using these lenses helps us to understand the consequences of adopting one policy or practice over another and, most importantly, helps us to be clear about whose interests are served by our choices. We begin with the assumption that these categories—race, class, and gender—are social constructions, not fixed and unchanging "realities," and that they intersect and interact with each other to refine our vision of the world. The best way to understand the full meaning of using an intersections approach is to recognize that there is no gender without race, no race without class, no class without gender. Taken together, these lenses shape our understanding of how our society functions. By focusing on new and constantly changing ways of defining difference, an intersections approach explores the multiple layers of social inequality and allows us to see how the layers play off each other to complicate rather than simplify the complex nature of personal identity.

That means that from the very start, so-called "personal identity" must be understood as a social construct. In place of the atomized individual that serves as the building blocks for political conservatism, the intersections approach begins with the assumption that a person's identity, which is to say their gender or their sexual identity, their race or ethnicity, their class background, and the privileges they enjoy or the ones that are denied them, can best be understood in terms of the social construction of reality. It is only by looking at the ways these categories intersect and impact on each other that we can arrive at a coherent understanding of reality. It also explains why sometimes the varied parts of our identity lead to conflict and confusion.

Another important assumption on which this book rests is that knowledge is positional. That means that knowledge is bound up with the knower's values and experiences and that there is a logical connection between thought and action. If I believe that knowledge implies action and the weather report tells me that severe flooding is predicted in my area, it's pretty clear that I *ought* to take certain actions in preparation. In the words of the philosopher and social thinker Karl Marx, our job is not merely to understand the world; our job is to change it!

And if we begin with the assumption that thought implies action, then it makes sense to use critical thinking to evaluate any idea or policy by asking ourselves what kinds of action this formulation of the problem is likely to lead to. For example, if we assume that tall people are less trustworthy than short people, it is likely that we will discriminate against tall people when deciding which applicant gets hired for a job. If we believe that criminal behavior is the result of innate character flaws, then it is more likely that we will incarcerate offenders rather than create programs for them that emphasize education and job training.

In addition to believing that social, political, and cultural categories are constructed in the course of political struggle and in response to changing circumstances, this books begins with the assumption that there are no individual solutions to what are essentially social problems and that only a comprehensive perspective, one that looks at how the intersections of race, class, and gender interact to shape our world, can provide the broad understanding we need. Once upon a time, problems were understood to be social in nature and we were encouraged to create policies that addressed them as such. For example, as sociologist Lynn Webber has pointed out, during the 1960s, poverty was understood to be a social problem, not an individual failing, and many teachers, scholars, and policy makers were determined to solve the problem of poverty. Instead of blaming poor people for their plight, our society challenged us to discover the social, economic, and political factors that needed to be addressed in order to make the United States more equitable. We looked at issues of race, class, and gender and how they interacted to both limit and define our reality in the interests of a small privileged class.

Published in 1963, at a time when America was celebrating its affluence, Michael Harrington's groundbreaking book, *The Other America,* described the lives of some 40 to 50 million people in this country who did not have adequate housing, education, or medical care. Harrington's subtitle, *Poverty in America,* made visible what had previously been invisible, and the book was responsible for this country committing itself to address these inequities. Soon after becoming president upon the assassination of John F. Kennedy, Lyndon Johnson declared a war on poverty, and as a result, programs such as Head Start, food stamps, work study, and Medicare and Medicaid were created. These programs, which used an intersections approach to understanding the nature of inequities and to come up with appropriate solutions, made a difference. Poverty rates went down and most poor people saw their standard of living improve. But since the 1970s, the poverty rate has stayed virtually the same and the wealth gap has grown significantly. Where we once had a war on poverty, most recently we have had a war on poor people.

In 2008 and 2009 we watched CEOs and hedge fund managers make enormous profits while the financial markets unraveled and millions of people lost their jobs, their homes, their life savings. At the very same time, a small number of the wealthiest individuals and the most powerful corporations found a way to profit enormously from the economic policy decisions, which reinforce rather than disrupt the prevailing distribution of power and privilege. How did we get to this point and whose interests are served by defining our problems in this way? Who is being bailed out and who went straight to the poor house?

For some time now, we have been encouraged to settle for answers that are intended to pacify us, to bring a halt to questioning rather than to critically evaluate the basic assumptions of our society—as critical thinkers ought to do. During the last Bush administration, talking about issues of race, class, and gender was considered "divisive" and was frowned upon. With the election of Barack Obama and the installation of a new administration, there was hope that things would change. A good place to begin the change is by asking whose interests are served by silencing discussion of difference. The severity of the recent economic crisis has made it imperative that we learn to think critically. The way to get beyond the reality of the differences in people's life chances because of race, class, and gender is not to pretend that these differences don't exist but to acknowledge them and then adopt and perpetuate policies and practices that change the structures of our society that produce the differences. That is what this text is designed to do. It begins with the assumption that by looking at how race, class, and gender are constructed and how they interact with each other, we will be in a better position to ask the right questions once again.

But asking the right questions can happen only if we begin by getting the facts right. How many of us know that the gap between the rich and the poor in the United States is the greatest among the industrialized nations of the world—and is increasing? How many working people know that the poor and the middle classes pay higher taxes than do the wealthy and that some of the wealthiest people and largest corporations in this nation pay little or no tax at all? How many of us know that 12.4% of the population live in poverty—that's 1 out of 8 people—and that the number of people living in extreme poverty—defined as 50% below poverty level—is steadily increasing, and most of these people are children? Is this the kind society we want? Is this the kind of global reality we want to perpetuate? Do we really want to throw in our lot with an economic system in which life expectancy, health, education, and even SAT scores are correlated with family income? Is it fair and just that the best predictor of future success is not hard work or ability or determination but your family's wealth? Initially, the Obama presidency held out the hope of a new way of thinking about our problems and new ways of addressing them, but only if we realize that these problems are built into the fabric of our society. Only if we recognize that privilege and inequality are not accidental consequences of arbitrary policies but are themselves structural in nature, that they have been built into the very policies and institutions of our society, can we begin to think critically about our choices and the policies and practices that deserve our support. Only learning to think critically holds out the hope of bringing about real change, change that is meaningful and longstanding and in the interests of the majority of people in our society.

In the end, the most disturbing gap for me, even more disturbing than the income gap, is the gap between what many people have mistakenly come to believe about our economic and social institutions in contrast to the actual lived reality of most peoples' lives. Thinking about the statistics we have just read should force us to wrestle with the truly difficult questions that underlie the foundations of this society, questions about extreme inequality with respect to income distribution and wealth, questions about opportunities for education and job training, access to health care and housing, transportation, and safety.

And of course that is what thinking critically is all about. Asking the right kinds of questions opens us up to a whole new set of issues and assumptions, many of which may have been obscured or rendered invisible by the belief system we have bought into unthinkingly or unintentionally. This belief system tells us repeatedly that America is the land of opportunity, that anyone who works hard can succeed, that discrimination based on race, class, or gender is a thing of the past, and that people who raise those issues are looking for excuses, not explanations.

Why are the inequities of class, race, and gender so difficult for many of us to see? Not only have we been taught a mantra that assures us that America is the land of opportunity and if we say it often enough it will become true, but we have been taught that today we live in a world where individualism reins supreme, where problems as well as solutions are defined in terms of individual accomplishments and failures. This emphasis on the individual, who sinks or swims by his or her own making, makes it impossible or unimportant to situate people in the context of their lives; it takes responsibility, yet again, away from the way our society is structured and places it firmly on the shoulders of the individual as if she or he were not a product of society and had no connection to it. By emphasizing the individual, we lose sight of the social dimension. We get lost among the trees and fail to see the forest. We ignore the interconnectedness of us all and we look for someone to blame rather than analyze the way our society is structured and the interests it serves.

What does it mean to understand problems as social rather than individual? Since this distinction is an essential part of what it means to think critically, let's take some time to be clear about it. A story that's been around a long time, often called the "Ogre Story," tells about a person who goes out for a walk along the river and sees a baby floating in the water. Naturally, he jumps in and pulls the baby to shore. But then he sees another baby floating down the river, and another. Calling for help, he is joined by others who follow him into the water and do what they can to save the babies. But this turns out to be an overwhelming task as more and more babies float down the river and need to be saved. Finally, the first man realizes that defining the problem in individual terms—saving the individual babies from drowning, one at a time—will never lead to a meaningful solution. What's needed is to find out why the babies end up in the river in the first place. I like this story because it so effectively distinguishes between doing a good deed—taking steps to make things better but without addressing the underlying causes of the problem—and engaging in social activism that tries to address the cause of the problem rather than merely addressing its symptoms.

Of course, sometimes a combination of the two is needed. Sometimes you need to deal with symptoms to buy time until you can focus on the cause itself. Obviously, you should take action to save the babies, but if you let that preoccupation prevail, you will find yourself on a road that leads to both exhaustion and defeat. Spending your time saving babies from downing is certainly admirable, but in the end what is needed is a long-term solution. Long-term solutions to social problems usually require structural changes in the way our society is organized. A good way to assess whether you are actually solving a problem or simply putting on a band-aid is to ask whether the proposed solution involves structural changes that are likely to have lasting, long-term effects. The most viable or satisfactory solutions will be ones that focus on the need to change policies and social structures and that involve people in working collectively to make a difference. That is the kind of social activism that can bring about real change.

Let's think a little more about what meaningful social actions look like. Recently, I received two e-mail messages urging me to "take action now." I ignored one and acted on the other. Why? The first was forwarded by a friend who urged all the recipients to participate in an online MSNBC poll that asked them to indicate whether or not they believed that "In God We Trust" should stay on America's currency. The person passing the message around reported that an overwhelming 85% of the people who responded said that the currency should remain the same; only 15% of those who responded voted in favor of its removal. My friend, who was surprised and disturbed by the lack of support for removing the line from our currency, urged everyone to vote. However, the request provided no framework in which I could think about the implications or the consequences of participating and it gave no context in which the poll was being taken, so the poll seemed to me to be in the same category as polls that ask, "Do blondes have more fun?" It was one more piece of mindless "news" that would appear on the Internet for a few hours and then disappear, to be replaced by yet another piece of mindless chatter.

The other e-mail message came from Amnesty International, a worldwide movement of people who campaign for internationally recognized human rights for all. According to their Web site, the organization has more than 2.2 million members in more than 150 countries and regions, and the organization coordinates this support to act for justice on a wide range of issues. The message reported that a research team recently found evidence of U.S.-made weapons in Gaza and urged Secretary of State Hillary Clinton to call for an immediate investigation into Israel's use of U.S. arms in Gaza. An accompanying page provided background information and provided a draft of the letter that was being circulated before being sent to Clinton.

These two e-mail messages and the actions they encouraged seem to me to provide a good example of what it means to be a critical thinker. In the first case, "voting" for either position really makes no difference because it has no substance. The person voting for or against the proposal might feel that they had "done" something, but the action was empty. Like so many similar acts, it creates the illusion of taking a stand but a stand on what? And why? In the second case, a problem is stated, relevant background is provided, and a form of action is proposed. This example illustrates what it means to do something that can be defined and evaluated as social activism. The first provides a person with the illusion of doing something meaningful, but the second is an example of what it means to engage in action with potential impact on policies and practice.

To this end, you might stop and read the articles in Chapter 2, "Does Shopping for a Good Cause Really Help? Activism and the New Chic." Like the e-mail example, the articles in this chapter provide good examples of how we can be misled into defining and "solving" a problem in a way that accomplishes nothing.

Another way that people have been taught to bring questioning to an end long before it is ready to stop and encouraged to settle for a nonanswer rather than continuing to ask hard questions is a technique that has come to be known as "blaming the victim." Sociologist William Ryan described it in his book of the same title. In it he points out that every important social problem—crime, mental illness, civil disorder, unemployment—has been analyzed and explained by reducing what is clearly a social problem to an individual issue. The framework that has been adopted is called the victim-blaming ideology. According to this way of thinking, it is the individual who is responsible for his or her own failure to get adequate education, health care, housing, and so on. Unlike the more blatant racism of the past, in this version it is the force of circumstance that produces people who are fated to be poor. It is the "culture of poverty" that is responsible. This framework explains what's wrong with the victim in terms of social experiences in the past, experiences that have left lasting wounds, defects, and disabilities. And the framework focuses on salving the wounds and reducing the disabilities as their first task. But to make this explanation acceptable, it is necessary to explain how the victims became vulnerable in the first place, and it is important, if this approach is to be successful, to do so without holding society at fault. Accordingly, this ideology blames the people themselves and attributes the problem to their apathy, ignorance, lack of education, failure to have better values. In the end, it is the victim who is responsible for her or his condition, not the unequal distribution of wealth and power and opportunity and resources. Not the corporations or the class system that make the rules, that builds white privilege and class and gender privilege into the way our society is structured and the policies and practices it favors. The victims have themselves to blame and everyone else gets a free pass.

To further illustrate what it means to think critically, let's take a look at the problems raised by the articles in Chapter 1, "Turning Your Lawn into a Victory Garden Won't Save You." All three articles focus on the so-called problem of hunger. Reminding ourselves that knowledge, if properly formulated, will lead to actions, what actions would defining the problem as "hunger" lead to? One author suggests that it is easy to define the problem in a way that leads us to settle for a series of band-aids rather than long-term solutions and urges us to take a broader and more constructive perspective by defining the problem not as hunger, but as poverty. Another article holds the corporations responsible, and another article goes even further and points to the way our political and economic systems are structured. In what ways do the articles propose different approaches to defining the problem and in what ways are they similar? How well does each of the ways push us to formulate questions that focus on the big picture, questions that are designed to provide answers that explain rather than excuse or obfuscate?

This book assumes that social problems require broad social solutions—not individual responses—and that learning to think critically to frame our questions and arrive at solutions will empower us as thinkers and activists. It assumes that what you don't know or can't see can definitely do you harm. To this end, this book seeks to make visible what is often invisible. Thinking critically and using the intersections approach encourages us to adopt a sophisticated worldview that begins with the understanding that identities intersect and interact and that a more complete understanding of our society and how to change it is possible.

The structure of this book illustrates the kinds of questions that critical thinkers raise. Each of the eight chapters consists of three articles, and each of the three articles examines a topic from a different perspective. Many books about critical thinking encourage readers to see the world in terms of whether they are for or against a particular issue, but the articles in this book cannot, for the most part, be understood in this way. Critical thinking is more complex than that. Reading the articles in the order in which they appear and then answering the questions at the end of each article provides the reader with firsthand experience of what it means to think critically. The questions and the order in which they are introduced are designed to make you aware of the ways in which we have been taught to see and not see the world. By leading the reader through articles and questions that assume very different approaches to framing a problem, this anthology disrupts the "mindless chatter" that has come to be mistaken for serious thinking and helps the reader recognize the difference between the two. From the first essay to the last, thinking through the questions will *show* you rather than *tell* you what it means to think critically.

I think you will find the answers interesting, and I hope you find this introduction to thinking critically useful. But it all begins with adopting the right framework and asking the right questions. What's the problem?

Turning Your Lawn into a Victory Garden Won't Save You

Chapter 1 of this book takes a hard look at the question of hunger in America and asks, "What's the problem?" Thinking about the articles in this chapter can help us understand what it means to frame a problem in a way that leads to a solution in terms of social action rather than to a dead end. An easy first answer to the question would have us look at the availability of food and the food supply, but the articles in this chapter reject naming hunger as the problem because defining the problem as hunger doesn't go far enough. It mistakes a symptom of the problem for the problem itself.

In Chapter 1, Stan Cox argues in the first article that "the big-commodity market must be not just modified but overthrown." He suggests that we must focus on the "political choke-hold that agribusiness has on the federal and state government" if we are to bring about the kinds of change that will empower people and put healthy food into their stomachs and into their lifestyle. As Janet Poppendieck observes, "defining the problem as hunger contributes to the obfuscation of the underlying problem of poverty and inequality." And further, as Frances Moore Lappé points out, we can end hunger forever but only if we empower our citizens to build democracies that are actually accountable to its citizenry. In short, as all three writers argue, we must be careful to define the problem in a way that focuses on overcoming privilege and moving closer to equality—rather than reinforcing privilege and inequality. If you solve the wrong problem you may have the illusion of success while perpetuating the very structures that create and reinforce what is at the root of the problem, institutionalized privilege and inequality.

Further Reading

DeLind, Laura B. "Celebrating Hunger in Michigan: A Critique of an Emergency Food Program and an Alternative for the Future." *Agriculture and Human Values,* Fall 1994, pp. 58–68.

Magdoff, Fred. "The World Food Crisis Sources and Solutions." *Monthly Review,* May 2008.

McMichael, Philip. "Global Food Politics," in Fred Magdoff, John Bellamy Foster, and Frederick H. Buttel, *Hungry for Profit* (pp. 125–144). Monthly Review Press, 2000.

Turning Your Lawn into a Victory Garden Won't Save You — Fighting the Corporations Will

Stan Cox

I didn't mean to lead anyone down the garden path. Adding my small voice to those urging Americans to replace their lawns with food plants wasn't, in itself, a bad idea. But now that food shortages and high costs are in the headlines, too many people are getting the idea that the solution to America's and the world's food problems is for all of us in cities and suburbia to grow our own. It's not.

Don't get me wrong: Growing food just outside your front or back door is an extraordinarily good idea, and if it's done without soil erosion or toxic chemicals, I can think of no downside. Edible landscaping can look good, and it saves money on groceries; it's a direct provocation to the toxic lawn culture; gardening is quieter and less polluting than running a power mower or other contraption; the harvest provides a substitute for industrially grown produce raised and picked by underpaid, over-sprayed workers; and tending a garden takes a lot of time, time that might otherwise be spent in a supermarket or shopping mall.

So it was in 2005 that our family volunteered our front lawn to be converted into the first in a now-expanding chain of "Edible Estates," the brainchild of Los Angeles architect/artist Fritz Haeg. We already had a backyard garden, but growing food in the front yard (which, as Haeg himself points out, is a reincarnation of a very old idea) has been a wholly different, equally positive experience.

Our perennials and annuals are thriving, we've gotten a lot of publicity, and I've been talking about the project for almost three years. Yet neither of our gardens, front or back, can stand up to the looming agricultural crisis. Good food's most well-read advocate, Michael Pollan, has written that growing a garden is worth doing even though it can make only a tiny contribution to curbing carbon-dioxide emissions. He might have added that growing food is worth it even if it does very little to revive the nation's food system.

"Turning Your Lawn into a Victory Garden Won't Save You—Fighting the Corporations Will," by Stan Cox, from AlterNet, June 23, 2008.

Reprinted with permission by Stan Cox.

World Cropland: The Pie Is Mostly Crust

The edible-landscaping trend is catching on across the country, and with food prices rising, it is taking sadly predictable turns. A Boulder, Colo., entrepreneur, for example, has tilled up his and several of his neighbors' yards and started an erosion-prone, for-profit vegetable-farming operation. It will supplement his income, but it won't make a nick in the food crisis.

That's because the mainstays of home gardening—vegetables and fruits—are not the foundation of the human diet or of world agriculture. Each of those two food types occupies only about 4 percent of global agricultural land (and a smaller percentage in this country), compared with 75 percent of world cropland devoted to grains and oilseeds. Their respective portions of the human diet are similar.

Suppose that half of the land on every one-acre-or-smaller urban/suburban home lot in the entire nation were devoted to food-growing. That would amount to a little over 5 million acres sown to food plants, covering most of the space on each lot that's not already covered by the house, a deck, a patio, or a driveway. (And in many places it couldn't be done without cutting down shade trees and planting on unsuitably steep slopes).

That theoretical 5 million acres of potential home cropland compares with about 7 million acres of America's commercial cropland currently in vegetables, fruits, and nuts, and 350 to 400 million acres of total farmland. The urban and suburban area to be brought into production would not approach the number of healthy acres of native grasses and other plants that are slated to be plowed up to make way for yet more corn, wheat, soybeans, and other grains under the newly passed federal Farm Bill.

A nationwide grow-your-own wave would send good vibes through society, ripples that could be greatly amplified by community and apartment-block gardening. But front- and backyard food, even if everyone grew it, would not cover the country's produce needs, much less displace our huge volume of fresh-food imports.

We could, instead, plant every yard to wheat, corn, or soybeans, which would account only for a little over two percent of the U.S. land sown to those crops. Other policies, like dispensing with grain-fed meat and fuel ethanol, would free up far more grain-belt land than that.

Not Even a Poke in the Eye

I've played a part in the promotion of domestic food-growing, and I now I seem to hear daily from people who believe that it's the best alternative to industrial agriculture (as in "I'll show Monsanto and Wal-Mart that I don't need their food!"). Even though most prominent home-lot food efforts, like the "100-Foot Diet Challenge," also try to draw attention to bigger issues, the wider message can get lost in the excitement. Whatever its benefits, replacing your lawn with food plants will not give Big Agribusiness the big poke in the eye that it needs, nor will it save the agricultural landscapes of the nation or world.

To do that, the big-commodity market must be not just modified but overthrown. Until then, most of that two-thirds or more of the human calorie and protein intake that comes from grains and oilseeds (directly in most of the world or among Western vegetarians, largely via animal products for others in this country) will continue to be served up by a dirty, cruel, unfair, broken system.

Essential for providing vitamins, minerals, and other compounds, a highly varied diet is important, and home gardens around the world help provide such a diet. But with a world population now approaching seven billion people and most good cropland already in use, only rice, wheat, corn, beans, and other grain crops are productive and durable enough to provide the dietary foundation of calories and protein.

Grains made up about the same portion of the ancient Greek diet [that] they do of ours. We've been stuck with grains for 10,000 years, and our dependence won't be broken any time soon.

The United States emulates Argentina and a handful of other countries by raising cattle that are totally grass-fed instead of grain-fed and thereby consuming less corn and soybean meal. But most of the world is utterly dependent on grains. The desperate people we saw on the evening news earlier this year, filling the streets in dozens of countries, were calling for bread or rice, not cucumbers and pomegranates.

Capitalism: It Doesn't Go Well with Food

Humanity's attachment to cereals, grain legumes, and oilseeds has acquired a much harder edge in the industrial era, but as a base for political and economic power, the staple grains have always been unsurpassed. Because [grains] hold calories and nutrients in a dense package that can be easily stored for long periods and transported, the more fortunate members of ancient societies could accumulate surpluses. Those surpluses are recognized by the majority of scholars as necessary to the birth of market economies, which allowed the prosperous to exercise control over society's have-nots.

Eventually, states used control over grains to exert political power over entire populations.

Few foods could have filled that role. Noting that before grain agriculture came along, ancient Egyptians might have gathered a surplus of various foods from nature, most of them highly perishable, economic historian Robert Allen once wrote, "If all a tax collector could get from foragers was a load of water lilies that would wilt by next morning, what was the point of having them?" The Pharaohs managed to exert control over the area's population only after people started farming wheat and barley.

The even bigger problem with grains—which are short-lived annual plants, grown largely in monoculture—is that they supplanted the diverse, perennial plant ecosystems that covered the earth before the dawn of agriculture. We've been living with the resulting soil erosion and water pollution ever since.

Then, when grains became fully commodified a couple of centuries ago, things really started to go downhill. In discussing his new book *Stuffed and Starved: The Hidden Battle for the World Food System,* Raj Patel cited India as an example: "The social safety nets that existed in India under feudal society had been knocked away by the British. If people couldn't afford food, they didn't get to eat, and if they couldn't buy food, they starved. As a result of the imposition of markets in food, 13 million people across the world died in the 19th century. They died in the golden age of liberal capitalism. Those are the origins of markets in food."

Indeed, if capitalism were a wine, it would be a wine that doesn't go well with any type of food.

Most food today is produced not as an end in itself but as a by-product of a global economy with the singular goal of turning maximum profit. That is a dysfunctional arrangement, as Nicholas Georgescu-Roegen, the founder of ecological economics, explained almost 40 years ago in his book *The Entropy Law and the Economic Process:* "So vital is the dependence of terrestrial life on the energy received from the sun that the cyclic rhythm in which this energy reaches each region on the earth has gradually built itself through natural selection into the reproductive pattern of almost every species, vegetal or animal. . . . Yet the general tenor among economists has been to deny any substantial difference between the structures of agricultural and industrial productive activities."

Industrial or commercial output can be increased by building more capacity, stepping up the consumption of inputs, taking on more workers, and pushing workers harder and for longer hours. Farming, by contrast, is inevitably bound by the calendar—by month-to-month variation in the capacity of soil and sunlight to support the growth of plants. It depends fundamentally on the productivity and the habits of non-human biological organisms over which humans can exert control only up to a point.

That clearly isn't the ideal pattern for efficient wealth generation, so the past century has seen relentless efforts to mold agriculture into the factory model as closely as possible and, where that can't be done, to graft more easily regimented industries—farm machinery, fertilizers, chemicals, food processing, the restaurant industry, packaging, advertising—onto an agricultural rootstock. In the US, the dollar outputs of those dependent industries are growing at two to four times the rate of agriculture's own dollar output, putting ever-greater demands on the soil.

With a wholesale shift toward mechanization of U.S. agriculture, 75 percent of economic output now comes from fewer than 7 percent of farms; furthermore, there has been a steep rise in the proportion of farms owned by investors living in distant cities (some of them perhaps avid urban gardeners).

Because, as Georgescu-Roegen showed, there's a fundamental difference between the farm and the factory, the well-used term "factory farming" represents more an aspiration than an accomplished fact. Nevertheless, agribusiness's attempts to defy natural rhythms and achieve industrial efficiency have been ecologically devastating. The biofuel craze, encouraged by subsidies that continue in the new Farm Bill, compounds the problem.

"We Must Cultivate Our Garden," and . . .

To repair the broken system that supplies the bulk of the nation's diet will require Americans to step out of the garden and into the public arena. Beyond working to get a better Farm Bill passed five years from now, we have to work together to break the political choke-hold that agribusiness has on federal and state governments.

With land and wealth being concentrated in fewer and fewer hands (and with more prisoners than farmers in today's America) we have actually reached a point at which land reform is as necessary here as it is in any nation of Latin America or Asia. Only when we get more people back on the land, working to feed people and not Monsanto, will the system have a chance to work. Most home gardeners know that the root of the problem is political, but the agricultural establishment would like nothing better than to see us spend all of our free time in our gardens and not in political dissent.

Ironically, it's that great troublemaker Voltaire who has too often been trotted out (and too often misquoted) as an advocate of withdrawing from the tumult of society, into tending one's own property. Voltaire was indeed a gardener, and he did end his most famous novel by having Candide, after surviving so many far-flung hazards, utter those famous words to his fellow wanderer, Dr. Pangloss: "We must cultivate our garden."

However, with the publication of *Candide* in 1759, Voltaire entered the most politically active part of his life, as he "went on to a series of confrontations with the consequences of human cruelty that, two hundred-odd years later, remain stirring in their courage and perseverance," in the words of Adam Gopnik.

If Voltaire could find the time for both gardening and radical political action, then all of us can do it.

Questions for 1.1

1. What does the author believe are some of the benefits of replacing your front lawn with a vegetable garden?
2. Why doesn't he believe that doing so is the solution to America's food crisis?
3. This article maintains that producing food is merely a by-product of the global economy. The real goal of the economy, according to Cox, is "turning maximum profit." How does Cox argue for his conclusion? What support does he provide for it?
4. Explain the author's reference to Monsanto.
5. Why does the author think that land reform is a necessary part of the solution to the current food crisis?
6. What does the author mean when he says that most gardeners know that the root of the problem is political?
7. According to the author, what is a more productive way to spend our time than working in the garden?

A Shortage of Democracy, Not Food

Frances Moore Lappé

What is killing democracy, while generating hunger? It is a belief system.

Forty years ago, squirreled away in the basement "Ag" library at U.C. Berkeley, I wanted answers to one question: Why were 960 million people going hungry?

At the time, newspaper headlines and experts from academia to the United Nations had their straightforward answer: Human numbers had hit the Earth's limits. But using my dad's slide rule, I put two and two together: Our "modern" farm economy was actively *creating* scarcity from abundance, in part by feeding a third of the world's grain to livestock.

Selection 1.2

I could hardly believe it. Could this Ph.D.-less twenty-something be right and the experts wrong? Stuffing my self-doubt, I composed a one-page handout. I assumed that if people just understood that hunger was needless, of course they'd get busy changing the economic rules creating it. The handout became *Diet for a Small Planet*.

I was right that hunger would worsen unless we dug to its roots. I was wrong, though, about what would happen next.

Four decades on, the World Food Program predicts the number of hungry people in the world will rise this year to what it was at that first Berkeley "a-ha!" moment.

Over these decades, the forces generating hunger from plenty have intensified. Food production has kept ahead of population growth, but now not only do we feed a third of grain and most of soy to livestock, but we've turned more than a third of the global fish catch into feed as well. Of course, I couldn't have guessed we'd also be "feeding" crops to cars via ethanol.

I'd hoped readers of *Diet for a Small Planet* would see this waste built into the post–World War II food system as only the surface layer explaining hunger. Beneath lies the deeper cause: the scarcity not of food but of *democracy*. Because no human being chooses hunger, hunger is proof that a person has been denied a voice in meeting survival needs. And, since a say in one's future is the very essence of democracy, the existence of hunger belies democracy.

"A Shortage of Democracy, Not Food," by Frances Moore Lappé, from *The Progressive*, July 2008. Reprinted with permission of Frances Moore Lappé; based on concepts from *Getting a Grip: Clarity, Creativity and Courage in a World Gone Mad*, Small Planet Media, 2007.

And what is killing democracy, while generating hunger? It is a belief system.

The belief is twofold: first, that an effective market works only by one rule, highest return to shareholder—that is, highest return to existing wealth; and second, that government is anathema to a market's effectiveness. From this stance, control over resources inexorably tightens to the point that it warps public decision-making to benefit narrow, private ends. We end up with a frightening oxymoron: "privately held government."

And from it flows what I call "faith-based economics" because it is detached from real-world evidence. History demonstrates that only a government accountable to citizens can keep a market competitive and open so that all citizens are able to access it.

Today's headlines, though, repeat the myth that weather and the inexorable increase in demand, especially among the new "middle classes" in India and China, explain the crisis—along with the unforeseen consequences of enlisting cropland in ethanol production. Wrong. Our worsening democracy deficit has continued to set the world up for disaster, undermining production and access to food worldwide.

Let us count the ways.

Unaccountable international agencies, including the World Bank and the International Monetary Fund, made loans on the condition that recipient countries reduce public support for local producers and food buyers. So African governments cut help to small farmers, and India said only the poorest of the poor could access its public "fair-price" shops that sell below-market-price grain.

Meanwhile, large agricultural interests in the North secured subsidies—almost half a billion dollars a day—making their grain so cheap its sales undercut markets for poor farmers in the South, ultimately driving many from the land.

And it gets worse. Trade agreements—most notably the 1994 North American Free Trade Agreement—ended tariffs that protected local farmers. In Mexico, for example, more than a million farmers went under in the decade following the agreement.

Then, in recent years, speculators have turned futures trading—set up to protect farmers and wholesalers from extreme weather-caused price swings—into their private bonanza, pushing up the short-term price of food.

Finally, while analysts talk as if the uptick in demand for wasteful grain-fed meat is inevitable, it isn't. Democracy deficits in India and China have generated massive inequalities, heightening demand for costly grain-fed meat.

With more equitable advancement that empowered rural dwellers, demand for meat could likely be met by small farms using the long-held, ecological, and cost-effective practice of feeding waste, like corn stalks and rice husks, to livestock.

The democracy crisis produces predictable and avoidable tragedy. But forty years later, what keeps me getting up in the morning is how much more we now know about sustainable growing and eating. We can turn today's tragedy into a breakthrough for common sense and real democracy as we:

- Get money out of—and citizens' voices into—governance.
- Shift public support to family farmers using sustainable agroecology. A 2007 University of Michigan study concluded that moving globally to sustainable, organic farming methods could increase food output by about 57 percent. A four-year study to evaluate the impact of such practices—involving almost thirteen million farmers and more than ninety million acres in fifty-seven countries—showed on average a 79 percent production increase.
- Grow the number of family farmers. One of the world's largest democratic social movements, Brazil's Landless Workers Movement, has succeeded in transferring almost twenty million acres to almost a third of a million rural landless families, creating thousands of new farmers and enterprises and greatly reducing hunger.

We can end hunger.

Forever.

We know how.

It depends, however, on citizens building confidence in their power to create democracies truly accountable to us.

Questions for 1.2

1. How did the author come to realize that our "modern" farm economy was actively creating scarcity from abundance 40 years ago?
2. Have things improved or gotten worse over the last four decades? Why?
3. According to the author, what policy choices and decisions have helped create the current food crisis?
4. What does the author mean by juxtaposing a shortage of democracy with the implied abundance of food? Is this an effective way to make the point?
5. Lappé maintains that the cause of the crisis can be traced to a belief system. Explain the nature of this belief system and how it is responsible for the shortage of food she describes.
6. What kinds of solutions does Lappé propose for ending hunger?
7. Is Lappé's approach to the current crisis similar or dissimilar to the concerns raised by Cox in the preceding article?

Want Amid Plenty: From Hunger to Inequality

Janet Poppendieck

"Scouting has some unacceptables," the Executive Director of the Jersey Shore Council of the Boy Scouts of America told me, "and one of them is hunger."[1] We were talking in the entrance to the Ciba Geigy company cafeteria in Toms River, New Jersey, where several hundred Boy Scouts, their parents, grandparents, siblings, and neighbors were sorting and packing the 280,000 pounds of canned goods that the scouts of this Council had netted in their 1994 Scouting For Food drive. The food would be stored on the Ciba Geigy corporate campus, where downsizing had left a number of buildings empty, and re-distributed to local food pantries to be passed along to the hungry. The

Selection 1.3

scouting executive was one of several hundred people I interviewed as part of a study of charitable food programs—so called "emergency food" in the United States. In the years since the early 1980s, literally millions of Americans have been drawn into such projects: soup kitchens and food pantries on the front lines, and canned goods drives, food banks, and "food rescue" projects that supply them.

Hunger Has a "Cure"

What makes hunger in America unacceptable, to Boy Scouts and to the rest of us, is the extraordinary abundance produced by American agriculture. There is no shortage of food here, and everybody knows it. In fact, for much of this century, national agricultural policy has been preoccupied with surplus, and individual Americans have been preoccupied with avoiding, losing, or hiding the corporeal effects of overeating. Collectively, and for the most part individually, we have too much food, not too little. To make matters worse, we waste food in spectacular quantities. A study recently released by USDA estimates that between production and end use, more than a quarter of the food produced in the U.S. goes to waste, from fields planted but not harvested to the bread molding on top of my refrigerator or the lettuce wilting at the back of the vegetable bin. Farm waste, transport waste, processor waste, wholesaler

"Want Amid Plenty: From Hunger to Inequality," by Janet Poppendieck, from *Hungry for Profit: The Agribusiness Threat to Farmers, Food, and the Environment,* edited by Fred Magdoff, John Bellamy Foster, and Frederick H. Buttel, Monthly Review Press, 2000.

Reprinted with permission by Janet Poppendieck.

waste, supermarket waste, institutional waste, household waste, plate waste: together in 1995 they totaled a startling 96 billion pounds, or 365 pounds—a pound a day—for every person in the nation.[2]

The connection between abundant production and food waste on the one hand, and hunger on the other, is not merely abstract and philosophical. Both public and private food assistance efforts in this country have been shaped by efforts to find acceptable outlets for food that would otherwise go to waste. These include the wheat surpluses stockpiled by Herbert Hoover's Federal Farm Board and belatedly given to the Red Cross for distribution to the unemployed, the martyred piglets of New Deal agricultural adjustment (which led to the establishment of federal surplus commodity distribution), and the cheese that Ronald Reagan finally donated to the needy to quell the criticism of mounting storage costs. Accumulation of large supplies of food in public hands, especially in times of economic distress and privation, has repeatedly resulted in the creation of public programs to distribute the surplus to the hungry. And in the private sphere as well, a great deal of the food that supplies today's soup kitchens and food pantries is food that would otherwise end up as waste: corporate over-production or labeling errors donated to the food bank, farm and orchard extras gleaned by volunteers after the commercial harvest, and the vast quantities of leftovers generated by hospital, school, government and corporate cafeterias, and caterers and restaurants. All of this is food that is now rescued and recycled through the type of food recovery programs urged by Vice President Al Gore and Agriculture Secretary Dan Glickman at their 1997 National Summit on Food Recovery and Gleaning. "There is simply no excuse for hunger in the most agriculturally abundant country in the world," said Glickman, who urged a 33 percent increase in food recovery by the year 2000 that would enable social service agencies to feed an additional 450,000 Americans each day.[3]

For Americans reared as members of the "clean plate club" and socialized to associate our own uneaten food with hunger in faraway places, such programs have enormous appeal. They provide a sort of moral relief from the discomfort that ensues when we are confronted with images of hunger in our midst, or when we are reminded of the excesses of consumption that characterize our culture. They offer what appear to be old-fashioned moral absolutes in a sea of shifting values and ethical uncertainties. Many of the volunteers I interviewed for my study told me that they felt that their work at the soup kitchen or food pantry was the one unequivocally good thing in their lives, the one point in the week in which they felt sure they were on the side of the angels. Furthermore, they perceive hunger as one problem that is solvable—precisely because of the abundant production—one problem about which they can do something concrete and meaningful. "Hunger has a cure," is the new slogan developed by the Ad Council for Second Harvest, the National Network of Foodbanks. It is not surprising, then, that hunger in America has demonstrated an enormous capacity to mobilize both public and private action. There are fourteen separate federal food assistance programs, numerous state and local programs, and thousands upon thousands of local, private charitable feeding projects which elicit millions of hours of volunteer time as well as enormous quantities of donated funds and food. In one random survey in the early 1990s, nearly four fifths of respondents indicated that they, personally, had done something to alleviate hunger in their communities in the previous year.[4]

The Seductions of Hunger

Progressives have not been immune to the lure of hunger-as-the-problem. We have been drawn into the anti-hunger crusade for several reasons. First, hunger in America shows with great clarity the absurdity of our distribution system, of capitalism's approach to meeting basic human needs. Poor people routinely suffer for want of things that are produced in abundance in this country, things that gather dust in warehouses and inventories, but the bicycles and personal computers that people desire and could use are not perishable and hence are not rotting in front of their eyes in defiance of their bellies. The Great Depression of the 1930s, with its startling contrasts of agricultural surpluses and widespread hunger, made this terrible irony excruciatingly clear, and many people were able to perceive the underlying economic madness: "A breadline knee-deep in wheat," observed commentator James Crowther, "is surely the handiwork of foolish men."[5] Progressives are attracted to hunger as an issue because it reveals in so powerful a way the fundamental shortcomings of unbridled reliance on markets.

Second, progressives are drawn to hunger as a cause by its emotional salience, its capacity to arouse sympathy and mobilize action. Hunger is, as George McGovern once pointed out, "the cutting edge of poverty," the form of privation that is at once the easiest to imagine, the most immediately painful, and the most far-reaching in its damaging consequences.[6] McGovern was writing in the aftermath of the dramatic rediscovery of hunger in America that occurred in the late 1960s when a Senate subcommittee, holding hearings on anti-poverty programs in Mississippi, encountered the harsh realities of economic and political deprivation in the form of empty cupboards and malnourished children in the Mississippi Delta. Hunger was in the news, and journalist Nick Kotz reports that a coalition of civil rights and anti-poverty activists made a conscious decision to keep it there. They perceived in hunger "the one problem to which the public might respond. They reasoned that 'hunger' made a higher moral claim than any of the other problems of poverty."[7] The anti-hunger movement—or "hunger lobby" that they initiated—was successful in enlisting Congressional support for a major expansion of food assistance and the gradual creation of a food entitlement through food stamps, the closest thing to a guaranteed income that we have ever had in this country.

The broad appeal of the hunger issue and its ability to evoke action are also visible in the more recent proliferation of emergency food programs. "I think the reason . . . that you get the whole spectrum of people involved in this is because it's something that is real basic for people to relate to. You know, you're busy, you skip lunch, you feel hungry. On certain levels, everyone has experienced feeling hungry at some point in the day or the year," explained Ellen Teller, an attorney with the Food Research and Action Center whose work brings her into frequent contact with both emergency food providers and anti-hunger policy advocates. The food program staff and volunteers I interviewed recognized the difference between their own, essentially voluntary and temporary hunger and hunger that is externally imposed and of unpredictable duration, but the reservoir of common human experience is there. Hunger is not exotic and hard to imagine; it stems from the failure to meet a basic and incontrovertible need that we all share.

Furthermore, the failure to eliminate hunger has enormous consequences. As the research on the link between nutrition and cognition mounts, the social costs of failing to ensure adequate nutrition for pregnant women and young children become starkly obvious. And this, too, contributes to the broad spectrum that Ellen Teller mentioned. There is something for everyone here—a prudent investment in human capital for those concerned about the productivity of the labor force of tomorrow, a prevention of suffering for the tender hearted, a unifying concern for would-be organizers, a blatant injustice for critics of our social structure. Many anti-hunger organizations with relatively sophisticated critiques of the structural roots of hunger in America have engaged with the "feeding movement," the soup kitchens and the food pantries, in the belief that, as the Bread for the World Institute once put it, "Hunger can be the 'door' through which people enter an introduction to larger problems of poverty, powerlessness, and distorted public values."[8] For those progressives seeking common ground with a wider range of American opinion, hunger is an attractive issue precisely because of the breadth of the political spectrum of people who are moved by it.

Third, progressives have been drawn into the hunger lobby by the utility of hunger as a means of resisting, or at least documenting the effects of, government cuts in entitlements. In the early 1980s, especially, when Ronald Reagan began his presidential assault on the nation's meager safety net of entitlement programs for the poor, progressives of all sorts pointed to the lengthening soup kitchen lines as evidence that the cuts in income supports, housing subsidies, food assistance, and a host of other public programs were cuts that neither the poor nor the society could afford. While Reagan and his team claimed that they were simply stripping away waste and fat from bloated programs, critics on the left kept track of mounting use of emergency food programs as a means of documenting the suffering caused by the erosion of the welfare state. The scenario is being replayed, this time amid an expanding economy, as soup kitchens and food pantries register the effects of "the end of welfare as we know it."

Finally, of course, progressives are drawn to the hunger issue by a sense of solidarity with those in need. Most of us became progressives in the first place because we cared about people and wanted a fairer society that would produce less suffering. Few of us can stomach an argument that says that we should leave the hungry to suffer without aid while we work for a more just future. "People don't eat in the long run," Franklin Roosevelt's relief czar Harry Hopkins is reported to have said; "they eat every day."[9] Many of the more activist and progressive people I interviewed in the course of my emergency food study articulated similar sentiments. A woman who worked in the early eighties helping churches and community groups in southern California set up soup kitchens and food pantries to cope with the fallout from the budget cuts in Washington recalled the dilemma as she had experienced it. "As far as I was concerned, the people in Washington had blood on their hands . . . but I wasn't going to stand by and watch people suffer just to make a political point." As one long-time left activist in Santa Cruz put it when questioned about her work as a member of the local food bank board, "There are numbers of people who are very compatible with my radical philosophy who also feel that foodbanking is very important, because the reality is that there are ever increasing homeless and poor, including working poor, who need to be fed . . . the need for food has increased and the resources for providing it haven't. And if there weren't foodbanks, I think a lot of people would starve."

It is easy to see why progressive people have been drawn into anti-hunger activity in large numbers, and why they have been attracted to the soup kitchens, food pantries, and food banks, despite misgivings about these private charitable projects. I, personally, have counted myself an anti-hunger activist since the nation rediscovered hunger in the late 1960s. Nevertheless, after three decades in the "hunger lobby," and nearly a decade of observing and interviewing in soup kitchens, food pantries, food banks, and food recovery projects, I would like to offer a caution about defining hunger as the central issue.

The Case Against Hunger

The very emotional response that makes hunger a good organizing issue, and the felt absurdity of such want amid massive waste, makes our society vulnerable to token solutions—solutions that simply link together complementary symptoms without disturbing the underlying structural problems. The New Deal surplus commodity distribution program, which laid the political and administrative groundwork for most subsequent federal food programs, purchased surplus agricultural commodities from impoverished farmers in danger of going on relief and distributed them to the unemployed already receiving public help. It responded to what Walter Lippmann once called the "sensational and the intolerable paradox of want in the midst of abundance," by using a portion of the surplus to help some of the needy, without fundamentally changing the basis for access to food.[10] As Norman Thomas put it in 1936, "We have not had a reorganization of production and a redistribution of income to end near starvation in the midst of potential plenty. If we do not have such obvious 'breadlines knee deep in wheat' as under the Hoover administration, it is because we have done more to reduce the wheat and systematize the giving of crusts than to end hunger.[11]

For the general public, however, the surplus commodity programs were "common sense," and they made well fed people feel better. Few asked how much of the surplus was being transferred to the hungry, or how much of their hunger was thus relieved. As the *New York Times* predicted in an editorial welcoming the program: "It will relieve our minds of the distressing paradox."[12] And with the moral pressure relieved, with consciences eased, the opportunity for more fundamental action evaporated. Thus the token program served to preserve the underlying status quo.

Something very similar appears to be happening with the private food rescue, gleaning, and other surplus transfer programs that have expanded and proliferated to supply emergency food programs since the early 1980s. The constant fund-raising and food drives that characterize such programs keep them in the public eye, and few people ask whether the scale of the effort is proportional to the scale of the need. With the Boy Scouts collecting in the fall and the letter carriers in the spring, with the convenient barrel at the grocery store door and the opportunity to "check out hunger" at the checkout counter, with the Taste of the Nation and the enormous array of other hunger-related fundraisers, with the Vice President and the Secretary of Agriculture assuring us that we can simultaneously feed more people and reduce waste through food recovery, with all this highly visible activity, it is easy to assume that the problem is under control. The double whammy, the moral bargain of feeding the hungry and preventing waste, makes us feel better, thus reducing the discomfort that might motivate more fundamental action. The same emotional salience that makes hunger so popular a cause in the first place makes us quick to relieve our own discomfort by settling for token solutions.

In the contemporary situation, the danger of such tokenism is even more acute. There is more at stake than the radicalizing potential of the contradictions of waste amid want. The whole fragile commitment to public income supports and entitlements is in jeopardy. Food programs not only make the well fed feel better, they reassure us that no one will starve, even if the nation ends welfare and cuts gaping holes in the food stamp safety net. By creating an image of vast, decentralized, kind-hearted effort, an image that is fueled by every fund-raising letter or event, every canned goods drive, every hunger walk, run, bike, swim, or golf-a-thon, every concert or screening or play where a can of food reduces the price of admission, we allow the right wing to destroy the meager protections of the welfare state and undo the New Deal. Ironically, these public appeals have the effect of creating such comforting assurances even for those who do not contribute.

Promoting hunger as a public issue, of course, does not necessarily imply support for the private, voluntary approach. There are undoubtedly social democrats and other progressives who support expanded food entitlements without endorsing the emergency food phenomenon. Unfortunately, however, much of the public makes little distinction. If we raise the issue of hunger, we have no control over just how people will choose to respond. As the network of food banks, food rescue organizations, food pantries, and soup kitchens has grown, so have the chances that people confronted with evidence of hunger in their midst will turn to such programs in an effort to help.

Many private food charities make a point of asserting that they are not a substitute for public food assistance programs and entitlements. Nearly every food banker and food pantry director I interviewed made some such claim, and the national organizations that coordinate such projects, Second Harvest, Food Chain, Catholic Charities, even the Salvation Army, are on record opposing cuts in public food assistance and specifying their own role as supplementary. When it is time to raise funds, however, such organizations, from the lowliest food pantry in the church basement to national organizations with high-powered fund-raising consultants or departments, tend to compare themselves with public programs in ways that reinforce the ideology of privatization. You simply cannot stress the low overhead, efficiency, and cost effectiveness of using donated time to distribute donated food without feeding into the right-wing critique of public programs in general and entitlements in particular. The same fund-raising appeals that reassure the public that no one will starve, even if public assistance is destroyed, convince many that substitution of charitable food programs for public entitlements might be a good idea.

Furthermore, as the programs themselves have invested in infrastructure—in walk-in freezers and refrigerated trucks, in institutional stoves and office equipment, in pension plans and health insurance—their stake in the continuation of their efforts has grown as well, and with it, their need for continuous fund raising, and thus for the perpetuation of hunger as an issue. While many food bankers and food recovery staff argue that there would be a role for their organizations even if this society succeeded in eliminating hunger, that their products also go to improve the meal quality at senior citizen centers or lower the cost of day care and rehabilitation programs, they clearly realize that they need hunger as an issue in order to raise their funds. Cost effectiveness and efficient service delivery, even the prevention of waste, simply do not have the same ability to elicit contributions. Hunger is, in effect, their bread and butter. The result is a degree of hoopla, of attention-getting activity, that I sometimes think of as the commodification of hunger. As Laura DeLind pointed out in her insightful article entitled "Celebrating Hunger in Michigan," the hunger industry has become extraordinarily useful to major corporate interests, but even without such public relations and other benefits to corporate food and financial donors, hunger has become a "product" that enables its purveyors to compete successfully for funds in a sort of social issues marketplace. It does not require identification with despised groups—as does AIDS, for example. Its remedy is not far off, obscure, or difficult to imagine—like the cure for cancer. The emotional salience discussed above, and the broad spectrum of people who have been recruited to this cause in one way or another, make hunger—especially the soup kitchen, food pantry, food recycling version of hunger—a prime commodity in the fund-raising industry, and a handy, inoffensive outlet for the do-gooding efforts of high school community service programs and corporate public relations offices, of synagogues and churches, of the Boy Scouts and the Letter Carriers, of the Rotarians and the Junior League: the taming of hunger.

As we institutionalize and expand the response, of course, we also institutionalize and reinforce the problem definition that underlies it. Sociologists have long argued that the definitional stage is the crucial period in the career of a social problem. Competing definitions vie for attention, and the winners shape the solutions and garner the resources. It is important, therefore, to understand the competing definitions of the situation that "hunger" crowds out. What is lost from public view, from our operant consciousness, as we work to end hunger? In short, defining the problem as hunger contributes to the obfuscation of the underlying problems of poverty and inequality. Many poor people are indeed hungry, but hunger, like homelessness and a host of other problems, is a symptom, not a cause, of poverty. And poverty, in turn, in an affluent society like our own, is fundamentally a product of inequality.

Defining the problem as hunger ignores a whole host of other needs. Poor people need food, but they also need housing, transportation, clothing, medical care, meaningful work, opportunities for civic and political participation, and recreation. By focusing on hunger, we imply that the food portion of this complex web of human needs can be met independently of the rest, can be exempted or protected from the overall household budget deficit. As anyone who has ever tried to get by on a tight budget can tell you, however, life is not so compartmentalized. Poor people are generally engaged in a daily struggle to stretch inadequate resources over a range of competing demands. The "heat-or-eat" dilemma that arises in the winter months, or the situation reported by many elderly citizens of a constant necessity to choose between food and medications are common manifestations of this reality.

In this situation, if we make food assistance easier to obtain than other forms of aid—help with the rent, for example, or the heating bill—then people will devise a variety of strategies to use food assistance to meet other needs. It is not really difficult to convert food stamps to cash: pick up a few items at the store for a neighbor, pay with your stamps, collect from her in cash. Some landlords will accept them, at a discounted rate of course, then convert them through a friend or relative who owns a grocery store. Drug dealers will also accept them, again at lower than face value, and you can resell the drugs for cash. The list goes on and on. Converting soup kitchen meals is almost impossible, but there are items in many pantry bags that can be resold. In either case, eating at the soup kitchen or collecting a bag from the food pantry frees up cash for other needs, not only the rent, but also a birthday present for a child or a new pair of shoes. By offering help with food, but refusing help with other urgent needs, we are setting up a situation in which poor people are almost required to take steps to convert food assistance to cash.

Conservative critics of entitlements will then seize on these behaviors to argue that poor people are "not really hungry." If they were really hungry, the argument goes, they would not resell items from the pantry bag or convert their food stamps. Such behavioral evidence fits into a whole ideologically driven perception that programs for poor people are bloated, too generous, and full of fraud and abuse; it allows conservatives to cut programs while asserting that they are preserving a safety net for the "truly needy." Progressives meanwhile are forced into a defensive position in which we argue that people are indeed "really hungry," thereby giving tacit assent to the idea that the elimination of hunger is the appropriate goal. In a society as wealthy as ours, however, aiming simply to eliminate hunger is aiming too low. We not only want a society in which no one suffers acute hunger or fails to take full advantage of educational and work opportunities due to inadequate nutrition. We want a society in which no one is excluded, by virtue of poverty, from full participation, in which no one is too poor to provide a decent life for their children, no one is too poor to pursue happiness. By defining the problem as "hunger," we set too low a standard for ourselves.

Where To?

The question of where we should direct our organizational efforts is inextricably tied up with the underlying issue of inequality. Above some absolute level of food and shelter, need is a thoroughly relative phenomenon. In an affluent society, the quality of life available at a given level of income has everything to do with how far from the mainstream that level is, with the extent to which any given income can provide a life that looks and feels "normal" to its occupants. In many warm parts of the world, children routinely go barefoot, and no mother would feel driven to convert food resources into cash to buy a pair of shoes, or to demean herself by seeking a charity handout to provide them. In the United States, where children are bombarded with hours of television advertising daily, and where apparel manufacturers trade on "coolness," a mother may well make the rounds of local food pantries, swallowing her pride and subsisting on handouts, to buy not just a pair of shoes, but a particular name brand that her child has been convinced is essential for social acceptance at the junior high school.

In this context, the issue is not whether people have enough to survive, but how far they are from the median and the mainstream, and that is a matter of how unequal our society has become. By every measure, inequality has increased in the United States, dramatically, since the early 1970s, with a small group at the top garnering an ever increasing share of net marketable worth, and the bottom doing less and less well. And it is this growing inequality which explains the crying need for soup kitchens and food banks today, even at a relatively high level of employment that reflects the current peak in the business cycle. Unfortunately, however, a concept like hunger is far easier to understand, despite its ambiguities of definition, than an abstraction like inequality. Furthermore, Americans have not generally been trained to understand the language of inequality nor the tools with which it is measured. Just what is net marketable worth, and do I have any? As the statistics roll off the press, eyes glaze over, and the kindhearted turn to doing something concrete, to addressing a problem they know they can do something about: hunger. Once they begin, and get caught up in the engrossing practical challenges of transferring food to the hungry and the substantial emotional gratifications of doing so, they lose sight of the larger issue of inequality. The gratifications inherent in "feeding the hungry" give people a stake in maintaining the definition of the problem as hunger; the problem definition comes to be driven by the available and visible response in a sort of double helix.

Meanwhile, with anti-hunger activists diverted by the demands of ever larger emergency food systems, the ascendant conservatives are freer than ever to dismantle the fragile income protections that remain and to adjust the tax system to concentrate ever greater resources at the top. The people who want more inequality are getting it, and well-meaning people are responding to the resulting deprivation by handing out more and more pantry bags, and dishing up more and more soup. It is time to find ways to shift the discourse from undernutrition to unfairness, from hunger to inequality.

Notes

1. All quotations not otherwise attributed come from the transcripts of interviews I conducted in conjunction with my study of emergency food. For a more extensive treatment, see Janet Poppendieck, *Sweet Charity? Emergency Food and the End of Entitlement* (New York: Viking, 1998).

2. Foodchain, the National Food Rescue Network, *Feedback* (Fall, 1997), 2–3.

3. Ibid.

4. Vincent Breglio, *Hunger in America: The Voter's Perspective* (Lanham, MD: Research/Strategy/Management Inc., 1992), 14–16.

5. For a discussion of the so-called paradox of want amid plenty in the Great Depression, see Janet Poppendieck, *Breadlines Knee Deep in Wheat: Food Assistance in the Great Depression* (New Brunswick, NJ: Rutgers University Press, 1986).

6. George McGovern, "Foreword," in Nick Kotz, *Let Them Eat Promises: The Politics of Hunger in America* (Englewood Cliffs, NJ: Prentice-Hall, 1969), viii.

7. Nick Kotz, "The Politics of Hunger," *The New Republic* (April 30, 1984), 22.

8. Bread for the World Institute, *Hunger 1994: Transforming the Politics of Hunger.* Fourth Annual Report on the State of World Hunger (Silver Spring, MD, 1993), 19.

9. Quoted in Edward Robb Ellis, *A Nation in Torment: The Great American Depression, 1929–1939* (New York: Capricorn Books, 1971), 506.

10. Walter Lippman, "Poverty and Plenty," Proceedings of the National Conference of Social Work, 59th Session, 1932 (Chicago: University of Chicago Press, 1932), 234–35.

11. Norman Thomas, *After the New Deal, What?* (New York: Macmillan, 1936), 33.

12. "Plenty and Want," editorial, *New York Times,* September 23, 1933.

Questions for 1.3

1. Why and how have so many people in America been able to mobilize around the issue of hunger?

2. What does Poppendieck mean by "the seduction of hunger"? And in what respects is she herself drawn to it?

3. What does Poppendieck mean by "the case against hunger"? Identify the three or four most persuasive observations she makes or state why you are unconvinced.

4. What does the author mean by "the commodification of hunger? Whose interests are served by this commodification?

5. Explain why the author believes that it is important to change the conversation from a focus on hunger to a focus on inequality.

6. Of the articles in Chapter 1, "Want Among Plenty" is the longest and offers the most complex arguments to support its conclusion. Evaluate the effectiveness of Poppendieck's argument and discuss the ways in which all three articles in this section agree and/or disagree with each other.

Does Shopping for a Good Cause Really Help? Activism and the New Chic

The articles in Chapter 2 illustrate the difference between defining the problem in a way that leads to social activism, which in turn is directed toward structural change, as opposed to a way that makes the real problem invisible. Chapter 2 examines the current trend toward encouraging us to think about the moral or ethical consequences of our shopping. Should we buy only eggs that are raised under humane conditions? Should we shop at stores or buy from designers or manufactures that give a portion of their profits to some "worthy" cause? In short, should we base our conscious decisions about what we buy and where we buy it on whether the manufacturers or the producers have made a commitment to "ethical shopping"? As the authors in Chapter 2 point out, shopping this way allows us to feel that we have "done something" on behalf of people or animals around the world that suffer the effects of poverty or illness or inhumane treatment, but the authors also ask whether shopping this way really makes a difference.

The three articles in this chapter and the questions that are posed after each article ask us to think critically about the broader questions and underlying issues raised by the approach we take. They ask us to think further about whose interests are served by defining activism in terms of "ethical shopping." Ethical shopping may make us feel good, but does it do anything to challenge or disrupt the inequitable distribution of power and privilege in our society? Does it ask us to rethink issues of profit and consumption and the way our economy is structured? Does it bring about the kind of structural changes that will have to be made if we want to change our priorities in ways that challenge inequality and move us toward shaping a different world?

Further Reading

Worth, Jess. "Buy Now, Pay Later." newint.org,/features/ 2006/11/01/ Keynote.

Worth, Jess. "Is Bono's Brainchild of Raising Money for the Fight against AIDS from Big Brands Inspi[red] or Ill Conside[red]?" Jess Worth interviews Tamsin Smith, Head of Product Red, and Sheila Roche, Red Director of Global Communications. *New Intrnationalist,* November 2006.

"Yes, There Is an ROI for Doing Good." *Advertising Age,* Adage.com, May 26, 2009.

The Rage Over (Red)

Jessica Bennett

Socially conscious marketing campaigns like Bono's "Shop for AIDS" are all the rage. But can shopping solve the world's problems?

When Ben Davis created buylesscrap.org, a quirky parody of Bono's (Red) campaign, he thought he'd get a few laughs out of his San Francisco designer friends. But since it launched two weeks ago, the site has received thousands of hits, hundreds of blog mentions—and has raised some very real questions about the spending practices and intentions of "cause marketing" campaigns like Red, which funnel a percentage of profits from the sale of consumer goods to charity. "A part of me was thinking long term about buying as a way to cure things, and feeling that was a bit manipulative," says Davis, who runs a creative marketing firm. "I think I put a voice to what many people were feeling."

Selection 2.1

Davis and his friends aren't the only ones questioning the "shopping to help charity" trend. An article in *Advertising Age* last week reported that since the campaign launched in the U.K. last March, its corporate sponsors (which include the Gap, Motorola and Apple, among others) have spent some $100 million on marketing but raised just $18 million for the Geneva-based Global Fund—one fifth less than a previously projected goal. Red cofounder Bobby Shriver called the marketing numbers (derived from independent analysts) "irresponsible journalism." Red says the actual value of the marketing is less than $50 million and that $25 million has been raised thus far, not the $18 million cited in the *AdAge* story. *AdAge,* meanwhile, stands by its story—saying that it derived its marketing total from three different "media experts' estimates of the marketing partners' outlay on print, TV, billboard and Internet ads, as well as the cost of a content-integration deal, in-store marketing materials and a pop-up store used by one of the partners."

Whatever the advertising figure, the debate over Red's model is bound to come up as a growing population of consumers try to help others while helping themselves to new T shirts and iPods. Activism is the new chic, and we, the consumers, have become the new activists—saving the world one credit-card transaction at a time. Cause marketing is a multibillion-dollar industry today (estimated to clock in at $1.4 billion in the United States this year—a growth of 23 percent since 2005, according to a study by the Chicago-based IEG Sponsorship Report), and it has carved out a niche within a group of young consumers who've grown accustomed to shopping for a cure. Ben & Jerry's American Pie encourages buyers to support its campaign to redistribute the federal budget to focus on children. Sun Chips are crunching for a cure for breast cancer, while Yoplait yogurt is saving lids to save lives—another cancer fund.

A 2006 survey by the marketing firm Cone Inc. found that 74 percent of American 13-to-25-year-olds are more likely to buy from a company with a strong commitment to a cause, while another survey, a collaboration between Cone and Alloy Marketing, found that in the past year, one in four college students has purchased a product because it was viewed as socially conscious. "Done appropriately, cause marketing does well with kids, with women, and with greens," says Paul Jones, a Salt Lake City-based marketing consultant who also authors the Cause-Related Marketing blog. "They think, 'If I'm already going to buy something, why wouldn't I buy the thing that gives back?'"

But how much are we really giving back? And when did shopping become the best way to help poor children in Africa? The Red folks would argue that any contribution is a good contribution, and that cause marketers are tapping into a group who may not donate otherwise, while also raising general awareness of issues such as AIDS and global poverty. Plus, they say, because corporations are benefiting, too, the product is more sustainable. "It's not that people say, 'Oh, I'm feeling charitable today, let me go to the Gap'," says Red's Shriver. "If you're feeling charitable, write a check. If you're feeling like you need a cool shirt, go to the Gap." So if you need to buy a pair of new sneakers anyway and you have a choice between a pair that helps only the manufacturer's pockets versus one that gives a percentage to a good cause, why not take the charitable route?

On the other hand, it isn't easy for consumers to determine the amount of their money going to charity. How much of that $28 for a Red Gap T shirt , for example, is actually making it into clinics and villages? Gap donates between 40 and 50 percent of its gross Red profits to the Global Fund—but that doesn't necessarily mean that 50 percent of your money is going there. Red won't reveal those numbers, but has an "impact calculator" that lets you see what your money can buy (a $28 shirt provides 41 single-dose treatments to prevent mother-to-child HIV transmission). But without knowing how the company calculates profit (after accounting for production, marketing, training, etc.), it's still unclear how many dollars are actually being sent to the Global Fund. If it's only 50 cents, would that affect your purchasing decision? "There's nothing wrong with corporations advertising, and there's nothing wrong with buying an iPod," says Randy Cohen, who writes "The Ethicist" column for *The New York Times* and is author of *The Good, the Bad & the Difference: How to Tell Right from Wrong in Everyday Situations.* "But there's something slightly deceptive if you think this is an effective way to address social problems." Gap did not return calls seeking comment.

David Crocker, author of *The Ethics of Consumption* and an international development expert at the University of Maryland, says we often don't realize the power of our purchases—and if we want to weigh the ethics of cause shopping, we must look not only at the quality of a good, but at its impact. That impact, he says, could be anything from environmental waste to poor working conditions. "What we buy and consume and use up and waste has a big impact on the developing world," he says. "So sometimes I think the responsibility is on the part of citizens to really take an active role [in learning about an item]."

But consumers might be understandably confused by advertising that looks charity-friendly but may not be. In its new ad campaign, Italian designer-denim brand Diesel has stuck a clan of models knee-deep in water on the rooftops of a flooded New York City—an obvious reference to the potential consequences of global warming or some other environmental disaster. The ad doesn't mention any benefit to environmental groups, though it does provide resources for more information, as well as questionable tips for what you can do (like have sex—to keep you warm and cut down heating bills). A Diesel spokeswoman says the campaign is an effort to get people thinking about climate change—and that the company does, in fact, contribute 10 percent of proceeds from a limited line of "wearable art pieces" (called the Diesel Denim Gallery) to Al Gore's Alliance for Climate Protection.

Barbara Brenner, the executive director of Breast Cancer Action, an education and advocacy group whose Think Before You Pink campaign is devoted to helping consumers understand the myriad of pink-ribbon products, sees "a transformation of public participation . . . into corporate America. . . . We've been encouraged as a culture to think we can solve problems this way, and there's pretty good evidence that it won't work."

Corporate America may be damned if they do and damned if they don't; they'll be criticized for not giving more but then critiqued when they try to find creative ways to do it. For Davis, transparency is key. "Maybe Red is a concept overreached," says Davis. "I think they've lost the faith of the broad sector of the cause-market, and the reaction to [my] very small site has shown that."

Questions for 2.1

1. Explain the "shopping to help charity" trend or, as it is also called, the "cause marketing" trend that is the subject of Bennett's article and give several examples of it.

2. What questions are raised for Ben Davis in this article when he talks about the unexpectedly large reaction to his parody of Bono's (Red) campaign?

3. What does Bennett mean by saying that "activism is the new chic"? Do you agree?

4. What does the author mean when she asks when shopping became the best way to help poor children in Africa? Should we take her questions seriously or does she ask them with a different intent?

5. According to this article, how much money has been spent by corporate sponsors of cause marketing and how much money has been raised for the Global Fund? Is this a good return on their investment?

6. What, according to David Crocker, who is quoted in the Bennett article, are some of the negative consequences of the shopping to help charity trend?

7. What is Jessica Bennett's answer to the question "Can shopping solve the world's problems?" Explain your answer.

Gift-Wrapped Guilt? My Adventure with Ethical Shopping

Frances Stead Sellers

Earlier this month, there was a three-day sale of imported Oriental rugs at the Mennonite church near my house in Baltimore. "They are a little pricey," one of my neighbors warned me wryly, "because the workers are paid a living wage." What a concept! The last time I bought an Oriental rug—years ago in Kashmir—I haggled over the price with little thought for the well-being of the rugmakers. I was pretty sure most of the profit would go to the store owner, anyway. But now my already stressful shopping season—garlanded with aspirations to find creative presents—had been complicated by the intrusion of al-truism: I was meant to worry about the workers.

Selection 2.2

So it was that I found myself watching another neighbor sort through piles of richly patterned, hand-knotted rugs, looking for just the right ruby tone to replace the threadbare floor covering in her dining room. She knew she probably wouldn't get a bargain that day, but she had been persuaded by the saleswoman's spiel that there was added ethical value to her purchase: Her investment would support Pakistani craftsmen and women (but no children, of course) who use looms donated by a charity, Jakciss, that is committed to building schools and promoting harmony between the country's Christian and Muslim populations.

I left the church with a warm feeling about an organization that was help-ing to maintain village life half a world away. But without a rug.

Buying a pricey Oriental would have been beyond my budget, I told my-self, and was not, therefore, the right thing for me to do. I'd check out some cheaper handcrafts instead, and other goods sold to support traditional arti-sans and farmers in the developing world. That decision pitched me, wallet-first, into the moral minefield of the movement known as "ethical shopping."

Using buying power to improve the world is a growing commitment among consumers in this country, according to the rug sellers at the Men-nonite church, who told me that increasing numbers of customers ask well-informed questions about the conditions under which their purchases had been made. And it has become big business in Europe, where a fair trade consumer guarantee was launched almost 20 years ago under the Dutch label Max Havelaar. The aim back then was to replicate the moral mindset that charities like Jakciss had fostered around niche handcraft markets and take it mainstream. According to the umbrella group Fairtrade Labelling Organizations International (FLO), there are now fair trade initiatives in 20 countries, including the United States, for such staples as cocoa, chocolate bars, orange juice, tea, honey, sugar and bananas as well as the ur-currency of the fair trade world—coffee. Between 2002 and 2003, sales of these goods grew by 42.3 percent worldwide. But there is also controversy brewing about just who's profiting from the guilt-charged spending habits of the Western world's consumers.

The pervasiveness of those habits came home to me a couple of months ago when I was in Britain (the world's largest fair trade market). My usually frugal brother sought out ground decaf coffee with the distinctive green and blue Fairtrade logo—and a higher price tag—for me at the Sainsbury's supermarket. Matthew told me he's prepared to pay more for fair trade "if a couple of pennies go to the poor grower," and he also tries to support people who grow produce locally in Cornwall, where he lives. But, he says, he's not holier-than-thou about his shopping, and he sometimes finds that his two goals conflict. He'll cast an eye over the ethical shopping reports that appear in London's newspapers now that the movement has picked up enough steam to cater regularly to people like him. The liberal *Guardian* reviews the Ethical Consumer Research Association's "best buys," which allocates each purer-than-the-driven-snow product a numerical "ethiscore."

The knowledge that people like my brother will pick fair trade products first off the supermarket shelves has prompted many stores to advertise the fact that they stock fair trade foods. And that has led, others suggest, to an indigestible melange of entrepreneurship and ethics.

That, at least, is the contention of conservative commentator Philip Oppenheim, who argued recently that in Britain, it's supermarkets that profit most from fair trade sales. They charge a premium for fair trade bananas, for example, while a "minuscule sliver ends up with the people the movement is designed to help," he writes. I'm not sure whether he's right. And that's the root of the problem: I'm a consumer, not a trade expert. I'm more interested in finding fresh fruit than in investigating profit margins as I swoop bananas into my shopping cart. But if he is right, Europe's experience may be a warning. A *Wall Street Journal* story last year, about misleading labeling by some companies here, said that Cafe Borders adjusted its pricing after it was suggested that the company might be taking advantage of consumers' charitable instincts.

If this modern, mainstream incarnation of fair trade is under attack from the right by those who believe that free trade is the fairest trade of all, it also risks a hammering from those on the left who feel that all big business is bad business. As Julian Baggini, who edits the British-based *Philosophers' Magazine,* put it, ethical consumerism "is characterised by three almost religious convictions: that multinationals are inherently bad; that the 'natural' and organic are inherently superior; and that science and technology are not to be trusted." So anti-globalization activists criticize huge companies such as Levi Strauss and Starbucks, even though Levi Strauss was among the first multinationals to establish a code of conduct for its manufacturing contractors and Starbucks is one of North America's largest roasters and retailers of fair trade coffee. And both can probably afford to be more altruistic than many smaller companies.

These days, Starbucks should be able to harvest a steady crop of customers with a thirst for fair trade coffee. TransFair USA, the California-based FLO member that certifies imports to the United States, reported a 91 percent increase in fair trade coffee imports into the United States—from 9.8 million pounds in 2002 to 18.7 million pounds in 2003—and a 76 percent increase the following year. When I went to a D.C. Starbucks on 15th and K Streets, near my office, I did find some green packets of Fair Trade Certified {+T}{+M} coffee beans tucked away at the back of a display stand, and they didn't cost any more than the other coffee. But when I ordered a cup of fair trade coffee, I was told there wasn't any—and that I was the first customer to have requested it. Perhaps K Street isn't the best place to look for ethically aware buyers, but Starbucks itself exudes a corporate philosophy brimming with goodwill: As Chairman Howard Schultz wrote in his 2004 report, a company "can do good and do well at the same time."

At this time of the year, some people I know have taken the idea of doing good by buying well to greater heights than I ever will. Over dinner a couple of weeks ago, a friend told me what he was planning to give his adult sons this Christmas: a heifer (to be donated to a family in the developing world by Heifer International, the charity whose goal is "Ending hunger, caring for the earth") and a bag of stone-ground cornmeal (from an 18th-century Pennsylvania grist mill, which is preserved as a museum "for the pleasure and education of the public").

Unlike my friend, I'm prepared to toss a little tinsel over my conscience and spend some money for fun instead of for socially responsible reasons. Still, I did buy toothpaste from Tom's of Maine (which donates 10 percent of profits and 5 percent of paid worker time to charity). I bought stocking stuffers from the Body Shop, whose founder, Anita Roddick, is savvy enough to leaven her company's earnest mission statement ("To dedicate our business to the pursuit of social and environmental change") with such sprightly scents as "Zest for Satsuma" and "Perfect Passion."

And I bought handmade soap (crafted from natural oils by traditional Indian soap makers) as well as folded paper Christmas ornaments (made by a group that supports disadvantaged Bangladeshis) from a special seasonal outlet of Ten Thousand Villages, which is the company that distributes the Jakciss rugs. And I enjoyed finding out more about the artisans on the company's informative Web site.

But I'm left with a conundrum. I want to do the right thing, but I'm not prepared to make a career of it. It's not hard to find criticisms online about the Body Shop, for example; it's much harder to verify them. And I'm much less interested in checking out the story behind the bananas I buy than I am in the origin of those origami ornaments. What's more, despite efforts by nonprofits like TransFair and the International Fair Trade Association or IFAT (which monitors companies like Ten Thousand Villages), there's a lot of room for misleading labeling in our ethical shopping baskets. So when it comes to my food shopping in particular, I'm left wondering whether I would be doing just as much good if I simply bought the best bargain and sent the money I had saved to a development charity (as Oppenheim would have me do). Best of all might be to buy locally whenever possible, like my brother.

Even the purchase that I believe was one of my most ethical is controversial. I bought a lamb. No, not a lamb like my friend's heifer, which will help feed a family in the developing world for years to come. My lamb will feed my already well-fed family in the weeks to come. I bought it—butchered and packaged for my freezer—from my daughter's old kindergarten teacher, who lives on a farm and used to bring orphaned lambs to school to be bottle-fed.

I can't pretend that I was motivated by the need to provide the workers with a living wage, although I do know that running a profitable business helps keep property taxes down and therefore keep the farmland open. No, I bought the lamb largely because the more I've read about the lives of animals that end up shrink-wrapped on supermarket shelves, the more I've developed a distaste for mass-produced meat. So it struck me as a principled stance to know that the animal I'm eating led a happy, hormone-free life, even if it was a short one.

But try telling my vegetarian friends that. Or even the carnivorous friends who came to dinner last Sunday and could hardly stomach the fact that I had such intimate knowledge of the creature I was carving.

One man's meat, you see, can be another man's ethical predicament.

Questions for 2.2

1. Why does the author leave the church with a warm feeling and what makes her buy some of the handicrafts made by traditional artisans and available for purchase at the church?

2. What prompts the author to ask, "Who's profiting from the spending habits of the Western world's consumers"?

3. Name some criticisms of the fair trade marketing movement made by people on the political right. Name some of the criticisms made by the antiglobalization activists on the left. What do you think of these criticisms?

4. Given how difficult it is to determine who profits from fair trade, what alternative does the author suggest? Do you think her possible "solution" is helpful?

5. Why does the author end her article by saying that "one man's meat is another man's ethical predicament"? What does she mean by ending the article this way?

Ethical Shopping Is Just Another Way of Showing How Rich You Are

George Monbiot

The middle classes congratulate themselves on going green, then carry on buying and flying as much as before.

It wasn't meant to happen like this. The climate scientists told us that our winters would become wetter and our summers drier. So I can't claim that these floods were caused by climate change, or are even consistent with the models. But, like the ghost of Christmas yet to come, they offer us a glimpse of the possible winter world that we will inhabit if we don't sort ourselves out.

Selection 2.3

With rising sea levels and more winter rain—and remember that when the trees are dormant and the soils saturated, there are fewer places for the rain to go—all it will take is a freshwater flood to coincide with a high spring tide and we have a formula for full-blown disaster. We have now seen how localised floods can wipe out essential services and overwhelm emergency workers. But this month's events don't even register beside some of the predictions circulating in learned journals. Our primary political struggle must be to prevent the breakup of the Greenland and West Antarctic ice sheets. The only question now worth asking about climate change is how.

Dozens of new books seem to provide an answer: we can save the world by embracing "better, greener lifestyles." Last week, for instance, the *Guardian* published an extract from *A Slice of Organic Life,* the book by Sheherazade Goldsmith—married to the very rich environmentalist Zac—in which she teaches us "to live within nature's limits." It's easy. Just make your own bread, butter, cheese, jam, chutneys and pickles, keep a milking cow, a few pigs, goats, geese, ducks, chickens, beehives, gardens and orchards. Well, what are you waiting for?

Her book contains plenty of useful advice, and she comes across as modest, sincere and well-informed. But of lobbying for political change, there is not a word. You can save the planet from your own kitchen—if you have endless time and plenty of land. When I was reading it on the train, another passenger asked me if he could take a look. He flicked through it for a moment, and then summed up the problem in seven words: "This is for people who don't work."

The media's obsession with beauty, wealth and fame blights every issue it touches, but none more so than green politics. There is an inherent conflict between the aspirational lifestyle journalism that makes readers feel better about themselves and sells country kitchens, and the central demand of environmentalism—that we should consume less. "None of these changes represents a sacrifice," Goldsmith tells us. "Being more conscientious isn't about giving up things." But it is if, like her, you own more than one home when others have none. Uncomfortable as this is for both the media and its advertisers, giving things up is an essential component of going green. A section on ethical shopping in Goldsmith's book advises us to buy organic, buy seasonal, buy local, buy sustainable, buy recycled. But it says nothing about buying less.

Green consumerism is becoming a pox on the planet. If it merely swapped the damaging goods we buy for less damaging ones, I would champion it. But two parallel markets are developing—one for unethical products and one for ethical products, and the expansion of the second does little to hinder the growth of the first. I am now drowning in a tide of ecojunk. Over the past six months, our coat pegs have become clogged with organic cotton bags, which—filled with packets of ginseng tea and jojoba oil bath salts—are now the obligatory gift at every environmental event. I have several lifetimes' supply of ballpoint pens made with recycled paper and about half a dozen miniature solar chargers for gadgets that I do not possess.

Last week the *Telegraph* told its readers not to abandon the fight to save the planet. "There is still hope, and the middle classes, with their composters and eco-gadgets, will be leading the way." It made some helpful suggestions, such as a "hydrogen-powered model racing car," which, for £74.99, comes with a solar panel, an electrolyser and a fuel cell. God knows what rare metals and energy-intensive processes were used to manufacture it. In the name of environmental consciousness, we have simply created new opportunities for surplus capital.

Ethical shopping is in danger of becoming another signifier of social status. I have met people who have bought solar panels and wind turbines before they have insulated their lofts, partly because they love gadgets but partly, I suspect, because everyone can then see how conscientious and how rich they are. We are often told that buying such products encourages us to think more widely about environmental challenges, but it is just as likely to be depoliticising. Green consumerism is another form of atomisation—a substitute for collective action. No political challenge can be met by shopping.

The middle classes rebrand their lives, congratulate themselves on going green, and carry on buying and flying as much as before. It is easy to picture a situation in which the whole world religiously buys green products and its carbon emissions continue to soar.

As many environmentalists argue, it is true that most people find aspirational green living more attractive than dour puritanism. But it can also be alienating. I have met plenty of farm labourers and tenants who are desperate to start a farm of their own but have been excluded by what they call "horsiculture": small parcels of agricultural land that are being bought up for pony paddocks and hobby farms. In places such as Surrey and the New Forest, farmland is now fetching up to £30,000 an acre as City bonuses are used to buy organic lifestyles. When the new owners dress up as milkmaids and then tell the excluded how to make butter, they run the risk of turning environmentalism into the whim of the elite.

Challenge the new green consumerism and you become a prig and a party pooper, the spectre at the feast. Against the shiny new world of organic aspirations you are forced to raise drab and boringly equitable restraints: carbon rationing, contraction and convergence, tougher building regulations, coach lanes on motorways. No colour supplement will carry an article about that. No rock star could live comfortably within his carbon ration.

But these measures, and the long hard political battle that is needed to bring them about, are unfortunately required to prevent the catastrophe that the recent floods presage—rather than merely playing at being green. Only when these measures have been applied does green consumerism become a substitute for current spending, rather than a supplement to it. They are harder to sell, not least because they cannot be bought from mail order catalogues. Hard political choices will have to be made, and the economic elite and its spending habits must be challenged, rather than groomed and flattered. The multimillionaires who have embraced the green agenda might suddenly discover another urgent cause.

Questions for 2.3

1. Why does George Monbiot say that shopping cannot bring about political change?
2. What does he mean when he says that green consumerism is another form of atomization?
3. What is Monbiot's main criticism of Sheherazade Goldsmith's recent book *A Slice of Organic Life*?

4. Why does Monbiot maintain that in the name of environmental consciousness we have simply created new opportunities for surplus capital?

5. All three of the articles in this section either implicitly or explicitly raise issues of class. What kinds of class issues are raised and what implications follow for issues of privilege?

6. What concrete examples does Monbiot provide of the kinds of hard policy choices we will have to make if we take green consumerism seriously?

3

It Didn't Happen and Besides, They Deserved It

The title of Chapter 3 is borrowed from Paul Loeb's powerful book *Soul of a Citizen*. The subtitle he chose, *Living with Conviction in a Cynical Time,* makes his purpose clear and gives us a clear idea of what it means to solve problems rather than wallpaper over them. Chapter 3 asks us to think about the problem of homelessness, its causes, and some possible solutions.

The first article by sociologist Lillian Rubin takes a broad view of the problem of homelessness and focuses on the way that large structural forces have changed the face of homelessness As Rubin argues, homelessness occurs not because the system doesn't work very well but because it is broken throughout the country. She maintains that the kind of dislocations and personal pain that are produced are the result of less, not more, government intervention.

The second article in Chapter 3, written by columnist C. Fraser Smith of the *Baltimore Sun,* explains that city officials at first operated on the assumption that calling attention to the problem of homelessness would be a bad thing. As with other problems, some people thought that the best way to solve the problem of homelessness was to ignore it. Calling attention to its existence would only aggravate the situation. Better to sweep it under the rug. But the Baltimore activists quoted in this article were committed to dealing with the problem, which they understood wouldn't be "solved" unless it was named. After considerable internal struggle, the activists agreed that the only way to approach the problem constructively was to recognize that homelessness must be addressed as one of a myriad needs that homeless people deal with throughout their lives. Not defining the problem in this way would only be contributing to the problem, not solving it.

In the final article in Chapter 3, "Hope for the Homeless?" the authors suggest that the problem of homelessness can only be solved by adopting a bold new housing policy. They suggest that how we understand and approach this crisis is critical to our ability to solve the problem of homelessness, and they point to a long history of failed federal housing policies that have led to this crisis. This brief article insists that we examine the current problem in light of its recent history and offers a sweeping solution. What do you think?

Further Reading

Burt, Martha. "What Will It Take to End Homelessness?" Urban Institute, September 2001.

"A Dream Denied: The Criminalization of Homelessness in U.S. Cities." NCH Fact Sheet, published by the National Coalition for the Homeless, June 2008.

Shinn, Mary Beth, et al. "The Prevention of Homelessness Revisted." *Analyses of Social Issues and Public Policy,* 2002, pp. 95–127.

Sand Castles and Snake Pits

Homelessness, Public Policy, and the Law of Unintended Consequences

Lillian B. Rubin

The walk from my home on top of San Francisco's Nob Hill down to my studio at its bottom is a lesson in class and status in America. As each few blocks take me down another rung on the socioeconomic ladder, I move from the clean, well-tended streets at the summit through increasingly littered, ill-kept neighborhoods where property values decrease as the numbers of potholes and homeless people increase. At the bottom of the hill sits the notorious "Tenderloin," a district that houses what the Victorians called "the lower orders," where the desperate and the dangerous hang on every street corner waiting for the local food kitchen to open its doors.

Selection 3.1

Three blocks later, I'm downtown looking at the visible signs of gentrification—an upscale shopping mall featuring the recently opened Bloomingdale's West Coast flagship store and an Intercontinental Hotel under construction next door. From there I pass into the more industrial parts of the city, where my studio sits in an old warehouse building, an entrance to the freeway on one corner and St. Vincent de Paul's homeless shelter—the biggest in the city—on the other.

How did this, the richest nation in the world, give birth to an enormous population of people who live on the streets or in shelters—men, women, and children, impoverished, desperate, and very often mentally ill? Three-quarters of a million Americans in 2005, the most recent national estimate, without a place to call home—a reckoning that most experts agree is far too low because it includes only those they could find to count. How did homelessness become so pervasive that a college student in the class on poverty in America I taught a few years ago couldn't conceive of a world without "the homeless"?

"Are you saying there didn't used to be homeless?" he asked, bewildered. "They've always been there, all my life," he continued, as other students nodded assent. How is it that even those of us who remember a time when homelessness was something that happened in India, not here in these United States, have become so inured to the sight of people living on the street that we walk past and around them without really seeing them?

"Sand Castles and Snake Pits: Homelessness, Public Policy, and the Law of Unintended Consequences," by Lillian Rubin, from Dissent, Fall 2007.

Reprinted with permission by Lillian Rubin.

Maybe it takes a few years of working next door to people without homes to see them, not as an undifferentiated mass—"the homeless"—but as men and women (mostly men) with whom I share a greeting when I arrive in the morning, people with names and faces and hard-luck stories. They're unclean, unkempt, and with a bone-deep weariness that seems to seep out of their pores, yet someone offers help when he sees me struggling to manage more than I can comfortably carry up the stairs. And once, when I tripped and fell, another picked me up off the sidewalk, wiped the blood off my face (never mind that he pulled a filthy rag of a handkerchief out of his pocket to do the job), and despite my protests, refused to leave until he saw me safely to my destination.

Homelessness in America isn't new, but it had a distinctly different flavor and meaning in earlier times. Then, homelessness was a transient phenomenon, generally tied to a sudden seismic event or the cycles of the economy. The Great Depression, for example, spawned a "hobo" population, mostly men from rural and urban communities who wandered from one part of the country to another in a fruitless search for work that didn't exist. But when the depression lifted and the economy brightened, they found jobs and homes. American cities, too, have always had pockets of homelessness, the skid row "bums" in neighborhoods like the Bowery in New York, "West Madison" in Chicago, the Tenderloin in San Francisco where the poor, the transient, the sick sought escape, and where alcoholics, still clutching the bottle, could be seen sleeping on the streets. But modern homelessness isn't just about "bums" or "hobos," nor is it confined to some small out-of-sight corner of the city. Instead, it's on our streets and in our face and, for those of us who live in any major city in the country, it's an inescapable fact of life.

They're black and brown and less often white; they're usually single and mostly men. For some being without a home is episodic, the result of an illness, an injury, a layoff, or for some of the women, domestic violence. The problem clears, and they're back on their feet—at least until the next time. But for hundreds of thousands of Americans, homelessness is a near-permanent, chronic condition from which there is currently no real escape.

The large structural forces that have changed the face of homelessness are no mystery: an increasingly stratified society with little opportunity for the unschooled and unskilled, a minimum wage that doesn't approach a living wage, unemployment and underemployment, cuts in public assistance, and urban rents that continue to rise well beyond what an unskilled worker can afford. But all of these together would not have created the scale of the problem we now face without the aid of two major public policy initiatives: the Housing Act, passed by Congress in 1949, and the Community Mental Health Centers Act, signed into law by President John F. Kennedy in 1963—good ideas with lofty goals, whose unintended consequences we see in the legions of homeless on the streets of our cities today.

In the landmark Housing Act of 1949, Congress declared that every American deserves a "decent home and a suitable living environment" and instituted a complex set of provisions to achieve that goal. For the growing post-World War II middle class, the increased authorization for the Federal Housing Administration (FHA) mortgage insurance (known as Title II) was a bonanza that helped millions realize the dream of homeownership. But for the poor, Title I, which called for an urban redevelopment program, became a disaster when its stated intent—to provide federal funds to upgrade decaying inner cities—fell victim to greedy local governments and the developers in their employ. Urban renewal, as it was known, soon became little more than an excuse for "poor removal" as bulldozers and wrecking balls demolished entire neighborhoods, some of them home to poor but vital communities, others featuring the shabby tenements, boardinghouses, and dilapidated hotels that offered single-room occupancy (SRO) housing to the poor, the lonely, the debilitated, the ill, and the drug addicts. And despite a provision (Title III) that committed the federal government to building 810,000 new public housing units—another policy that experience has shown created at least as many problems as it solved—local, state, and federal governments looked the other way as urban renewal, with its promise of increased land values, quickly came to replace concerns for housing, and far more living units were destroyed than were built.

This isn't to say that urban renewal was a failure for everyone. Not by a long shot. Parts of many inner cities did, indeed, become more attractive, as blighted neighborhoods were cleared for such amenities as hotels, shops, cultural centers, and even small patches of green. But in the game of winners and losers, it's no surprise that only the poor lost. The developers lined their pockets. Local governments reaped the reward of increased land values as the new steel, concrete, and glass towers attracted business that brought jobs and revenue to the city. The glossy high-rise condominium buildings that rose in place of rundown homes, tenements, and SROs brought the affluent, who had fled to the suburbs decades earlier, back to the city where they could now live in style and comfort while enjoying the convenience of having Macy's, Neiman Marcus, a bank branch, and the city's cultural offerings at their doorstep. Only the poor and the sick were left with no place to go, except into the streets or the public housing projects that now look and are more like prisons for the poor than the "decent home and suitable living environment" Congress declared as every American's right.

Lest anyone think urban renewal is a thing of the past, I'll be happy to take them on a tour of the projects under way in my hometown of San Francisco or, if that's too far to go, to direct them to a *New York Times* article of June 16, 2007, whose opening words tell the story: "For nearly three decades, Charlotte Johnson witnessed the drug dealing and violence on the streets in front of her modest row house in East Baltimore. She rode it out only to face a new challenge today—the community's transformation under the largest planned urban renewal in the country, which could soon drive her out of the neighborhood."

Step back to the past again, to 1963 and the Community Mental Health Centers Act, a historic piece of legislation whose good intentions would set the stage for yet another social debacle. The American mental health reform movement has a long and not very successful history. In 1868, after Elizabeth Packard was released from an asylum to which her husband had committed her some years earlier, she founded the Anti-Insane Asylum Society and published a series of pamphlets describing her experiences. Shocking as her tale was, her entreaties for public attention fell on deaf ears, because most people then still believed that madness was the result of demonic possession.

Forty years later, Clifford W. Beers's *A Mind That Found Itself* was somewhat more successful in stimulating public interest, but it would be several more decades before *The Snake Pit,* a film starring Olivia de Havilland, opened in 1948 to a stunned American audience. Everyone knew, of course, that there were insane asylums, places where crazy people were locked up so the rest of us could sleep easily at night. But it is testimony to the power of film that the visual images woke the American conscience in ways that hundreds of thousands of written words had not. Suddenly, the "insane" were not just some undifferentiated mass, they were women and men hidden from view in human warehouses, held in the care of sadistic guards, shackled to walls in dungeonlike cells, and subjected to torturous "treatments"—immersed in tanks of ice water, spun in chairs for hours, secluded naked in isolation rooms, restrained in straitjackets or cuffed hand and foot to a bed in spread-eagled position, force-fed medications, shocked with high volts of electricity to the brain, and lobotomized—all by psychiatrists who knew little about the cause or relief of their symptoms.

Still, the mental health reform movements didn't gain any real traction until the mid-1950s, when the development of psychotropic medications gave promise of symptom relief, if not a cure, for some of the worst of the mental ailments. Although the new drugs were not without significant, and often dangerous, side effects, thousands of patients were taking them, and, by the end of the decade, people who would once have been committed to asylums for life were managing to live outside them and tell their stories.

The hope the new medications brought, coupled with the various rights movements that were roiling society in the 1960s, set the stage for the emergence of a vigorous patients' rights movement, led largely by former hospital patients and their families. They offered a stinging critique of institutional psychiatry that was instrumental in discrediting the practices and treatments that had turned hospitals into snake pits, called for an end to involuntary commitment, and demanded that patients have a voice in their treatment.

The presidency of John F. Kennedy gave the reform movement a big lift when his family made their private pain public with the announcement that a family member had been mentally ill and institutionalized for years. With increasing pressure from the reformers and the backing of a sympathetic president, Congress passed the Community Mental Health Centers Act in 1963, which sought to create an alternative to institutionalization in state mental hospitals by developing a system of mental health centers that would focus on preventive, community-based outpatient care.

What happened? It's always easier for the federal government to spell out good ideas than it is to put up the hard cash necessary to make them work. So perhaps the simplest explanation is that the road to hell is paved with unfunded and underfunded government programs. Still, there's rarely a single cause to explain either the success or failure of a policy initiative.

As the social and political background changed in the decades following the passage of the Community Mental Health Centers Act, the good intentions that brought it into being faded away. The Vietnam War was a continuing drain on the public purse. Tax revolts and antigovernment ideologies of both the right and the left blossomed in the 1970s, which, together with the recession of the early 1980s, further weakened both the government's coffers and its resolve. Ronald Reagan's election to the presidency in 1980 turned a budding conservative movement into a full-scale revolution that changed the American social and political landscape for decades to come. All these played a part in restricting federal funding for social programs, including mental health, so that by the mid-1980s the regional funding model the 1963 law promised—never enough even at the beginning—was scaled back, and mental health services shifted once again to state and local levels until now, when federal funds support only about 2 percent of total state mental health budgets.

But long before federal funds dried up, the states played their part in turning a good idea into a fiasco. Until the new law, mental health care was the province and the burden of the states. When the federal government entered the picture with a plan for community care and the promise of funds to support it, it was a gift that offered states relief from the enormous financial costs of supporting a large hospitalized patient population. Not surprisingly, therefore, state and local officials spoke the language of mental health advocacy and community care, but they acted on their concern for fiscal policy. Without waiting for the promise of the law to become a reality, they jumped on the deinstitutionalization bandwagon and transferred tens of thousands of mentally ill women and men, many who had spent years in confinement, to communities that had no way to support their care.

Before long, the few Community Mental Health Centers (CMHCs) that existed were overwhelmed by demands they simply couldn't meet. It was a devastating experience for both the patients and the professionals. "We had no choice but to turn people out into the street," one veteran of the time recalls. "The state hospital, the place of last resort, was gone; there were no halfway homes, no treatment programs, nothing." Yet deinstitutionalization continued, ultimately closing nearly half the hospitals in the country and dramatically reducing bed capacity in those that are left, leaving uncounted tens of thousands of people to fend for themselves.

Although thousands of deinstitutionalized patients made a more or less successful transition to life outside the hospital, living with families or in adult group homes where they existed, many others fell through the cracks—and are still falling. For serious mental illnesses such as schizophrenia and bipolar disorder are not a one-time problem that can be cured with a pill. Even patients who seem to be doing well need regular monitoring and counseling if they're not to slip and fall. Moreover, welcome as each new generation of psychotropic drugs has been, they are no free lunch for the men and women who must live on them to maintain their sanity. For, along with the gift of gaining some control over the delusions of schizophrenia or the excessive mood swings of bipolar disorder, come side effects that can range from such discomfiting problems as weight gain and blurred vision to serious and sometimes irreversible neuromotor difficulties with Parkinsonian symptoms that can disfigure a life.

In addition to physical side effects that can be almost as disabling as the disease itself, drugs that alter the mind also alter consciousness in ways that challenge a person's experience of self. Patients often complain that they "feel different," that, as one person said to me some years ago, "I feel like a stranger to myself"—feelings that drive a very large proportion of the mentally ill to stop taking the drugs, which inevitably throws them into crisis.

Ask any family with a schizophrenic or bipolar member, and you'll hear stories about the weird and sometimes dangerous behavior that suddenly appears when the patient secretly stops taking medication. Listen to them speak of the difficulty of finding their way through the chaotic maze of uncoordinated public agencies that is now our mental health system, only to fail because there are no beds or community services available. Hear their agony as they describe what it's like to find a loved one living on the street and be helpless to do anything about it.

In the recent uproar about the Virginia Tech shootings, the executive director of the Virginia Commission on Mental Health Reform was asked why a young man who had been diagnosed as "mentally ill and in need of hospitalization" wasn't either hospitalized or closely monitored in an outpatient setting before he walked onto the campus and killed thirty-two people. His reply? "The system doesn't work very well." An understatement of breathtaking proportions.

Whether homelessness or crazed killing sprees, they don't happen because "the system doesn't work very well," but because it's broken, not just in Virginia but throughout the land. The Virginia Tech shooter wasn't closely monitored by mental health professionals because, whatever the services his community may say it offers, there simply are never enough resources or staff to provide them. Homelessness isn't an accident or an artifact of some strange modern urban disease, but a product of failed social policy. It got its first big push when urban renewal destroyed poor neighborhoods without offering adequate housing alternatives. Deinstitutionalization shoved it even harder when the plan to provide community-based mental health services turned out to be an empty promise, starved of funds even before the first patients were sent off to find their unsteady way into communities that had no services or facilities for them. And while all this was happening, the patients' rights movement won victories in the legislatures and the courts (including the United States Supreme Court in 1999 in *Olmstead* v. *L.C.*) that make it virtually impossible to hold someone with serious and sometimes dangerous mental problems involuntarily for more than a few days without proof, certified by a court, that the person is an immediate threat to society and/or to self—a test that isn't easy to meet absent violence or proof of intent to commit it.

"You think it's a problem, just try living with it," sighed the director of a clinic with whom I spoke recently about the mental health problems of the homeless. "We try, but we don't have the staff or the resources. And even if I could find a bed for some of the worst of them—which, frankly, I usually can't—if they don't want to go, the law won't let me hold them for more than seventy-two hours no matter how crazy they are. So what's the point? You knock yourself out to find a place where maybe, just maybe, they can get help, and a couple of days later, they're back out on the street."

True, but even for those who are amenable to treatment, the best any mentally ill homeless person is likely to get these days is a bed to rest in just long enough for the doctors to find the right drug regimen to stabilize a crisis. After that he or she is back out into the community with no services, no follow-up, and no place to live—a revolving door that never stops turning.

The result? About 500,000 of the 750,000 homeless Americans, men and women who are sick, desperate, and without hope, presently live in shelters or on the streets because of some form of mental illness. Yes, there are other social and economic forces that have contributed to the rise of homelessness. But the virtual epidemic we know today wouldn't exist without the fallout from two historic public policy initiatives: the Housing Act of 1949 that set urban renewal in motion and the Community Mental Health Centers Act of 1963 that sought to reform the mental health system—both well-intentioned, if flawed, good ideas that fell victim to the law of unintended consequences.

Do we conclude then that good intentions don't matter, that, as conservatives would have it, it's the nature of government to make a mess of even the best ideas, and that, therefore, we need less and less government intervention, no matter what the intent? I don't think so. True, government is not always as efficient as we'd like it to be. It's too cumbersome, too often unprepared for the unforeseen consequences of its actions, too slow to correct its mistakes, and our legislators are too often more beholden to special interests than to the common good. But even in a pluralist democracy like ours, where legislation is the product of compromise and negotiation that can subvert the framers' good intentions, it doesn't always happen that way, as the Social Security and Medicare programs aptly demonstrate. Not that they're perfect, not that the compromises made to ensure their passage haven't left their mark. But compare the successes of the original single-payer Medicare program to the recent Medicare Prescription Drug Benefit—a complicated bureaucratic nightmare that relies on the private sector to provide insurance. Despite the fact that our costs exceed anything government-insured programs spend in countries that offer better, cheaper, and more complete drug coverage, Medicare Part D, as the drug benefit is known here, has brought far more benefit to the insurance companies and their pharmaceutical allies than to the old and the sick.

How, then, do we avoid the unintended consequences that can cause the kind of social dislocation and personal pain I've described here? Perhaps we can't; perhaps it's in the nature of the system—any system—that we can't always foresee the pitfalls until we tumble into them. But the problems of legislation such as the Medicare Prescription Drug Benefit should remind us that it isn't government's attempts at reform that need to be curbed but the influence of corporate America on the legislative process. Indeed, recent experience—the turn to the private sector for what earlier had been part of the public trust, the many revelations of corporate malfeasance, greed, and incompetence—suggests that only the willfully blind can continue to insist that the government has no place in reform and that the private sector will always do it better and cheaper.

Questions for 3.1

1. What, according to this article, is the difference between the kind of homelessness that was typical the United States in the past and the kind of homelessness that exists now?

2. How did this, the richest nation in the world, give birth to an enormous population of people who live on the streets or in shelters—men, women, and children, impoverished, desperate, and very often mentally ill?

3. What are some of the structural forces that can explain this change?

4. What, according to this article, is the relationship between urban renewal and the rise in homelessness?

5. What is the relationship between mental health reform and the increase in the numbers in the homeless population?

6. Why does the author maintain that "hopelessness . . . is a product of failed social policy"? Be as specific as you can.

7. How well does Rubin explain homelessness and how successful is she in arguing that the public sphere, not the private, should assume a leadership role in this area? Agree or disagree and support your opinion.

"Everyone Deserves a Place to Sleep at Night"

C. Fraser Smith

In the beginning, city officials asked these homeless activists if they could avoid calling attention to themselves: no high-visibility signs or big lettering at the front door of the old bank building they had rented. This was back in the day when critics of help for the homeless had a kind of reverse *Field of Dreams* view of things: If you don't build a refuge, they said, maybe they won't come.

If you don't address the problem, in other words, maybe it'll go away.

The lettering on the window outside the old Equitable Bank Building at 111 Park Ave. still doesn't demand attention. But the problem didn't go away. Street people had their ways of communicating. They got to know where they could go for help.

Nor did Jeff Singer and the handful

Selection 3.2

of men and women who work with him go away. They have shown several generations of Baltimore leaders how the city might demonstrate care and compassion for men, women and children who sleep under expressway ramps and in churchyards.

They have done their work with such relentless avidity that official Baltimore, once anxious for them to disappear, has become a champion. The state has become a partner as well, allotting $3.7 million for the program over the years. Private citizens and various charitable organizations are raising $15.5 million for a new facility. Of this about $14 million is in hand, so the fundraising continues.

Thus on Thursday, city and state officials will be on hand to inaugurate a new Health Care for the Homeless center at the corner of Hillen Street and the Fallsway.

"It's kind of amazing to us," says Mr. Singer, a social worker and social change agent. "People told us we'd never be able to raise the money. We weren't big enough. We didn't have enough of a base. But we persisted."

Mr. Singer's persistence and profile have become legend. He's been as quiet a champion as any member of the establishment could want. With his navy blue tam, his head and face haloed in white hair, he smiles as if the world will always come around to his way of thinking.

"'Everyone Deserves a Place to Sleep at Night,'" by C. Fraser Smith, from the *Baltimore Sun*, August 8, 2008.

Reprinted with permission by C. Fraser Smith.

And so it has. Mayor Sheila Dixon recently announced a 10-year plan to end homelessness. She stood her ground against the naysayers with this observation: "Everyone deserves a place to sleep at night."

Former Baltimore mayor, governor and comptroller William Donald Schaefer became an advocate. Never one to offer government help until people demonstrated their own commitment to an idea or a project, he saw Mr. Singer's quiet passion. At one point, he came and sat in the program's waiting room, just observing the system. As governor, he put the program in his budget, thereby conferring important financial stability.

Health Care for the Homeless now lives in the same warren of offices it moved to 17 years ago on Park Avenue. Its original three-member staff has grown to 127. It has three psychiatrists and eight therapists. The old bank building is so crowded that three outreach workers have desks in an old vault bristling with wheels and bars. It's an airless warren that succeeds in pushing these workers onto the street in search of clients.

Health Care for the Homeless last year had 54,000 visits from the estimated 8,000 homeless people in Baltimore. The clinic addresses myriad medical needs. It did 1,000 tests for HIV last year, finding more than 100 people who were HIV-positive and in need of treatment.

Not wishing to leave the matter in the hands of individuals with such transient and erratic lifestyles, the center includes a place where patients can come to take their medications.

Homelessness, Mr. Singer says, is simply a symptom of poverty, with the lack of low-cost housing and jobs at the root of it. Most of the people who seek help at the clinic have no health insurance. Some have lost their jobs as a result of the economic downturn—and, earlier, more homeless were produced by the cutback in benefits that occurred with welfare reform.

Given the nation's economic distress, these issues are not likely to be addressed in the near future. The need for Mr. Singer's program will undoubtedly grow even as he joins those who wish there was no need. Mr. Singer and his team observe that even with a conservative national administration, new initiatives—triggered in part by the economic slowdown will address some of the underlying problems.

So, this Thursday, ground will be broken for the new building near the feeding program Our Daily Bread and near Mercy Hospital, which deals with Jeff Singer's sicker clients.

A sign on the front of the new health center will proudly say, in letters large enough to be seen from the nearby expressway, Health Care for the Homeless.

Questions for 3.2

1. Who said, "Everyone deserves a place to sleep at night"?

2. What might the speaker have meant by using the word "deserves"? In what sense might he make that claim? Agree or disagree and explain your position.

3. To what, according to Singer, is homelessness attributable?

4. How has the city of Baltimore responded to homelessness?

5. In the introduction to this book, a distinction is made between solutions that depend on charity and solutions that depend on social activism. Which of these categories is more appropriate for the solutions posed by this article?

6. In the end, Smith is generally optimistic about Baltimore's ability to solve the problem of homelessness in the city. Is his optimism justified? Explain your answer.

7. How would you describe the way Singer and his colleagues have brought about change in Baltimore?

Hope for the Homeless?

Patrick Markee and Lizzy Ratner

With homeless rates at record highs, America needs a bold new housing policy.

On January 14, as the combined forces of recession and foreclosure continued their long, cruel assault on the Rust Belt, Cleveland's public school system marked the new semester with a troubling piece of data: the number of students who had been homeless at some point during the school year had jumped to 1,728. Compared with the same date in 2006, this number represented a spike of nearly 150 percent and served as further confirmation that, for all the [whining] of Wall Street executives, the poor and vulnerable have been hardest hit by the flailing economy.

Selection 3.3

Not that Cleveland's poorest students needed reminding. In December, when Project ACT, a social service program for homeless students run by the Cleveland Metropolitan School District, asked a group of homeless parents what they wanted for Christmas, the parents responded with wish lists worthy of *Little Dorrit*: toilet paper, bleach, paper towels, food.

"We figured they'd be asking for some nice things, [but] they were asking for basic, basic household things," said Marcia Zashin, Project ACT's director. "Times are tough. They're very tough."

Such are the stories pouring out of schools and homeless shelters these days, evidence of a crisis that many fear is bound to get worse. Throughout the country, homelessness is rising, with ever more families in ever more towns and cities sleeping in shelters, surfing friends' couches and camping in their cars. In San Bernardino, California, for instance, the City Unified School District counted roughly one-third more homeless students in the 2007–08 school year than in the previous one, part of a stomach-churning trend that has pushed the number of homeless students in the state past 224,000, according to local officials. In Boston the number of families without homes shot up 22 percent, from 3,175 in December 2007 to 3,870 in December 2008. And in New York City, which shelters an astonishing 36,000 homeless people each night (including nearly 16,000 kids), the number of newly homeless families entering the shelter system hit an all-time high in autumn, with the influx in November 44 percent higher than the previous year. Along the

"Hope for the Homeless?" by Patrick Markee and Lizzy Ratner. Reprinted with permission from the March 14, 2008, issue of *The Nation*. For subscription information, call 1-800-333-8536. Portions of each week's *Nation* magazine can be accessed at http://www.thenation.com.

way, the total number of homeless families bedding down each night in shelters topped 9,700—the highest number since the city began keeping records more than twenty-five years ago.

By most accounts, there's little mystery to this rise in the ranks of shelter seekers. It's the economy and, more specifically, the recession and the foreclosure crisis. As people have lost their paychecks, or as the homes they were renting were foreclosed—most of today's homeless foreclosure victims are renters who were evicted, even though they paid rent, because their landlord had not kept up with the mortgage—their tenuous grip on stability has slipped away. And many housing experts think this could be just the beginning. Because the recession is far from over; because the unemployment rate hit 7.2 percent in December and is expected to climb; because the foreclosure crisis has more misery to dole out; and because homelessness is a lagging indicator—families tend to cling to their homes as long as they can, forgoing food, clothes and medication just to keep their roof—the number of homeless families will likely continue to spike.

But there's another essential point, one that bears fundamentally on how we understand—and tackle—this crisis. While the recession has swollen the ranks of the homeless population, modern homelessness has been with us for more than a quarter-century. Long before subprime mortgages, credit default swaps and the most recent stock market crash, the United States was in the grip of the longest period of sustained mass homelessness since the Great Depression. Indeed, even before the current economic downturn some 3.5 million Americans (including 1.4 million children) experienced homelessness during the course of a year. For this we can thank not a periodic dip in the business cycle but an affordable-housing crunch spawned by nearly three decades of slash-and-burn housing policy.

Just as the Wall Street meltdown can be traced to the deregulate-at-any-cost ideology of the Reagan years, modern homelessness and the widening housing affordability gap were fostered in the Gipper's free-market nursery. From the earliest days of his administration, Reagan set about systematically dismantling federal housing programs, slashing funds for federal rental vouchers and public housing. He also initiated the shift in federal low-income housing policy away from subsidized development to tax-credit programs, which fail to help the poorest families. The reason was pure conservative hocus-pocus: the idea that housing is a commodity best created and priced by the unregulated, unfettered market and that government should play little or no role in guaranteeing shelter to its poorest citizens.

During the next decades, this ideology never disappeared, and it enjoyed a particularly virulent renaissance in George W. Bush's America. Even as the Bush administration made a show of doling out small increases to the homeless services budget (though never enough to meet the need), it hacked away at public housing, Section 8 vouchers and other housing programs, undermining any attempt at reducing family homelessness. Indeed, since 2004 funding for affordable housing programs has declined by $2.2 billion. The result is a country in which only one in four eligible low-income households receives federal housing assistance while those forced to go it alone, without any government assistance, face an increasingly harsh landscape of rising rents and declining wages. It's no wonder the number of poor renters paying more than half their income for rent rose by more than 1 million households, or 29 percent, between 2001 and 2007.

Fortunately, we have a chance to rewire the country's housing policy, an opportunity born of the start of Barack Obama's administration and a climate made more receptive to public investment by the awful imperatives of the economic meltdown. More than at any time in recent history, this moment calls for the kind of visionary and dramatic action too rarely seen from leaders—certainly not Republicans but also many Democrats, who have spent much of the past two decades fidgeting on the margins of federal housing programs.

There are a lot of ways President Obama could begin tackling such a challenge—including a bold and unequivocal commitment to ending homelessness once and for all. As another critical first step, the Obama team (including New York City housing commissioner Shaun Donovan, who is expected to be confirmed as the new head of the Department of Housing and Urban Development) and Congress can adopt a $45 billion proposal, drafted by the National Low Income Housing Coalition and forty other progressive policy groups, as part of the stimulus package. This plan is premised on years of academic research: that the best way to solve homelessness is to provide people with homes—to create permanent supportive housing (i.e., affordable housing with support services) for people living with mental illness and other special needs and to offer affordable housing assistance (in the form of vouchers or low-income housing) to homeless families.

Toward this end, the plan calls for a minimum of 400,000 new rental vouchers as well as a $10 billion infusion over two years in the recently created National Housing Trust Fund—a move that would jump-start construction of badly needed low-cost homes. To help address more imminent needs, the plan suggests expanded aid for victims of foreclosures and another

$2 billion for vital homelessness prevention services. Additional investments of $15.4 billion would address the long-neglected upkeep of public housing and help these and other subsidized developments "go green" by improving energy efficiency. Taken together, these initiatives will help more than 800,000 vulnerable households and create more than 200,000 jobs.

Of course, cleaning up the wreckage of three decades of failed federal housing policy will take more than one stimulus; these measures are just the beginning of what's needed. But if change is the order of the day, dismantling the Reagan-Bush legacy of modern homelessness would be a promising way to start.

Questions for 3.3

1. How should we understand the housing crisis?
2. How does this article explain the current increase in homelessness? Do the authors maintain that it is a result of subprime mortgages, credit default swaps, and the recent stock market crash, or is there another explanation?
3. What, according to the authors, has caused the current housing crisis?
4. What kind of evidence do they present in support of their claims?
5. What is the relationship between the free market and the Wall Street meltdown?
6. What role did the ideology adopted by Ronald Reagan and George W. Bush play in exacerbating the crisis? Be specific.
7. What evidence do the authors present to convey the severity of the housing crisis? Is it persuasive?
8. According to the authors, what are some of the initiatives that will help address this crisis? Be specific.

Poverty Is Hazardous to Your Health

Chapter 4 examines the problem of poverty with special attention to its impact on health issues. The first article is critical of politicians who merely give out band-aids rather than getting down to the difficult job of solving the health crisis. The United States is the only nation in the industrialized world that doesn't provide some kind of health insurance for its population. Caught between conservatives, who look to private insurers, and liberals like the late Ted Kennedy, who press for a single-payer plan, most people are left feeling confused and uncertain about where their interests lie. Offered a choice among placebos, they understandably don't know which choice to make.

In the second article, columnist Katha Politt looks at the health crisis from the point of view of health care professionals as well as ordinary people, who must navigate the perilous waters and stay afloat while providing some degree of health care for themselves and their dependents. As her article demonstrates, this is not an easy task.

The third selection in Chapter 4, "Inequality: Bad for Your Health," reprints an interview with social epidemiologist Ichiro Kawachi. His solution to the health crisis requires nothing less than creation of a relatively egalitarian society. Rejecting the prevailing conversation, which, as he points out, focuses almost entirely on how to ensure health coverage for everyone, Kawachi broadens the questions and reframes the problem to be solved. He suggests that the public debate about heath needs to include a discussion of economic policies and must occur within the context of the multidimensional context that recognizes the connection between a person's health and the quality of the person's life in which the health issues play themselves out. He suggests that many of these problems can change dramatically when the gap between rich and poor increases.

Unlike the first two articles, which try to arrive at solutions within the political and social realities of the day, the third article demonstrates what happens when the thinker steps outside the box and reframes the problem entirely. Does his approach offer us a useful example of critical thinking?

Further Reading

Goodrich, J. "Talk to Me Like I'm 4: Why Our Health Care System Failed Us and How We Can Fix It." *Alternet,* February 12, 2009.

Marmor, Theodore. "Universal Health Insurance." *Dissent,* Summer 2007.

World Bank. "Poverty and Social Impact Analysis: Lessons and Examples from Implementation," 2007.

Health Policy Placebos

David U. Himmelstein and Steffie Woolhandler

We don't administer useless nostrums for curable cancer—even when effective treatment is arduous. Yet Hillary Clinton and Barack Obama prescribe the health policy equivalent of placebos. (John McCain suggests arsenic, but more about him another time.)

The Democratic contenders proffer a superficially plausible reform model that has a long record of failure. Their proposals trace back to Nixon's 1971 employer mandate scheme, concocted to woo moderate Republicans away from Ted Kennedy's single-payer plan. Like mandate reforms subsequently passed (and failed) in Massachusetts (1988), Oregon (1989) and Washington (1993), Clinton's and Obama's plans would couple subsidies for the poor with a requirement that large employers foot part of the bill for employee coverage.

Selection 4.1

These earlier reforms also required the self-employed to buy coverage, an individual mandate that Clinton (like the 2006 Massachusetts reform) would expand to virtually all; Obama limits his mandate to children. In both versions, a federal agency would serve as insurance broker, selling a new public plan and a menu of private ones—reprising the format of Medicare's ongoing privatization, implemented through competition rigged to favor private plans [see Trudy Lieberman, "The Medicare Privatization Scam," *The Nation*, July 16/23, 2007].

The earlier state reforms foundered on the shoals of cost. As health spending soared, employers rebelled and legislators rescinded the mandates and subsidies. Massachusetts looks set to replay this experience; only 7 percent of those required to buy unsubsidized coverage have yet to sign up, while the state wrestles with massive cost overruns for subsidies.

Proposals that rely on private insurers can add coverage only by adding costs. Both Democrats promise savings from computerization, prevention and chronic disease-care management. Yet medical computing hasn't yielded savings, despite thirty years of rosy promises. As for prevention, a raft of studies show that it saves lives but not money. And the Medicare Health Support program recently abandoned its care management project because it yielded no savings.

Both Democrats' proposals forgo the administrative savings possible under single-payer national health insurance (NHI) such as that proposed by the

"Health Policy Placebos," by David U. Himmelstein and Steffie Woolhandler, from *The Nation*, March 14, 2008. Reprinted with permission from the March 14, 2008, issue of *The Nation*. For subscription information, call 1-800-333-8536. Portions of each week's *Nation* magazine can be accessed at http://www.thenation.com.

Conyers/Kucinich bill (HR 676) and by Ralph Nader. Bureaucracy consumes 31 percent of US health spending, versus 17 percent in Canada. The difference translates into $350 billion frittered away annually here, where a million healthcare workers, as well as hundreds of thousands in the insurance industry, spend their days on useless paperwork.

This waste is a natural byproduct of private insurance. Private plan overhead is eleven times that of Canada's NHI program. Each dollar spent on private premiums buys only 88 cents of care; the rest pays for insurers' marketing, underwriting, utilization reviewers and profits—and for the billions paid to their CEOs. Fragmented coverage also means duplication of claims processing facilities and mountains of paperwork for doctors and hospitals, which must deal with multiple insurance products each with its own eligibility rules, co-payments, referral networks, etc.—tasks that are absent in Canada. Our multiplicity of insurers also precludes the payment to hospitals of a global, lump-sum budget. In Canada global budgets obviate the need for most hospital billing and much of the internal accounting needed to attribute costs to individual patients and payers.

Clinton's and Obama's plans also lack credible means to redirect the hundreds of billions now wasted on overtreatment. Hospitals, doctors and equipment firms profit from investments in expensive high-tech care, encouraging the overuse of interventions that help some patients but harm others—for example, spine surgery, cardiac stents and CAT scans (which often deliver radiation equivalent to 500 chest X-rays). Insurers limit their outlays through intrusive case-by-case reviews or by raising co-payments. But they have little interest in systemwide cost control, so their efforts have mainly shifted costs to patients or other payers—the economic equivalent of squeezing a balloon. In contrast, NHI would allow explicit public decision making about today's capital investments that shape tomorrow's care, and straightforward mechanisms to limit profit.

Without savings, the tax increases Obama and Clinton propose would be eaten up by subsidies for the uninsured, leaving nothing for the majority of Americans already covered but often unable to afford care. As we found in a 2005 study with Elizabeth Warren and Deborah Thorne, three-quarters of the 750,000 families driven to bankruptcy each year by illness or medical bills had coverage, though with unaffordable co-payments, deductibles and uncovered services. NHI would eliminate these gaps.

Private insurers caused the healthcare crisis. Yet both Democratic contenders advocate reforms that would fortify private plans, making government their debt collector. Their proposals, while palatable to the health industry—which supplies the Democrats with huge donations as well as key officials (DNC credentials committee co-chair James Roosevelt moonlights as an insurance company CEO)—cannot cure our healthcare crisis.

Nonetheless, we're optimistic about the prognosis for healthcare reform. If you turn up the volume on C-SPAN you can hear the audience cheering whenever Clinton or Obama lets the words "single payer" slip out—a reflection of the fact that three-fifths of the general public, as well as the 124,000-member American College of Physicians, support NHI. As in the JFK era, a charismatic, if only tepidly liberal, candidate can help raise hopes and expectations, igniting a mass movement that pushes a progressive agenda further and faster than the candidate intends.

Questions for 4.1

1. What is a placebo? Give two or three examples.
2. What, according to the authors, is wrong with proposals for health insurance that rely on private insurers?
3. What are the benefits of a single-payer approach?
4. What is the likelihood of savings from medical computing?
5. Why is the Canadian NHI more cost effective than the system in place in the United States?
6. According to this article, what caused the health care crisis?
7. According to the authors, do the Republicans and Democrats have similar or dissimilar interests when seeking to solve the problem of how to provide health insurance for the population?
8. What is the source of optimism for health care reform?

Poverty Is Hazardous to Your Health

Katha Pollitt

The four of us were just about to sit down to a delicious end-of-summer dinner of grilled pork ribs and corn on the cob when the phone rang. It was for my friend, Dr. Michele Barry, Yale medical school professor and chief of one of the teaching wards at Yale-New Haven Hospital, who was on call that weekend. "Tell me what's the matter," she said into the receiver, using her reassuring, unfazable doctor voice. "Hmm-hmm. And how long has this been a problem?" Michele left the room briefly to continue the conversation, and when she came back she was in full exasperated-at-the-system mode. The patient, mother of a month-old baby, was crying on the phone because for the past

two days she had been tormented by head lice (*Pediculosis capitis,* if you really want to know). A simple problem, you might think—head lice is endemic among schoolchildren, as many a parent could tell you—and one that hardly needs a high-powered medical consultation. You just go to the drugstore, buy a bottle of Nix (permethrin) over the counter and spend a lot of time with that little plastic comb. But Nix costs $22.99, and this woman didn't have it. By then it was Saturday night, and the drugstores in her neighborhood were closed until Monday. Fortunately, there was an all-night pharmacy, so Michele prescribed her permethrin, which Medicaid would pay for. She does the same thing for women with yeast infections who can't afford $16 for the over-the-counter Monistat: She prescribes terazol (a much more expensive medication), which is covered by Medicaid.

You can see this incident as a tiny illustration of the penny-wise, pound-foolish complexities of our bizarre healthcare system, in which routine problems are treated as full-blown emergencies, and the government will pay for prescriptions but not over-the-counter medications that may be cheaper and work just as well. The President asserted that there's no healthcare crisis, because anyone can just go to the emergency room if they need care. He's wrong—ERs don't give ongoing or preventive treatment; they just patch you up in a crisis. But to the extent that ERs and free services like Yale's have become the family doctor or the CVS for low-income people, that *is* the problem, because they're incredibly expensive. This is the system its defenders claim we must keep because single-payer health insurance would bankrupt the nation.

But this is also a story about the way poverty and health are intertwined. If you are reading this, chances are good that you can put your hands on $22.99. It's not a huge amount of money—it's pizza and beer for two, a hardcover book, two tickets to the movies. But there are a lot of people like Dr. Michele's patient, for whom $22.99 might as well be $122.99. They just don't have it when they need it. Even the co-pays on lifesaving prescription drugs can be too much for them. "I have patients who say to me that they can't afford to get both the diabetes and the heart meds, so they're just getting one this month," says Dr. Mark Cullen, also a Yale professor of medicine, and Dr. Michele's husband.

Forget, too, the other things so necessary to good health that the rest of us take for granted. Fresh fruits and vegetables—try even finding these in an inner-city neighborhood. Clean air—poor neighborhoods are notoriously the most polluted. Safe streets. Housing in good repair. A life with no more than the ordinary amount of stress. Well, you'd be stressed out too if you couldn't afford to get rid of your head lice. What else can't Dr. Michele's patient afford if she can't afford that? Try school supplies and books for her child in a few years. Try vitamins and a good breakfast every morning.

We hear a lot these days about the struggles of the middle class. Remember M2E2—Medicaid, Medicare, education, environment—the mnemonic New Democrats adopted after the Republicans took Congress in 1994? Except for the minimum wage, even progressives now routinely frame their policies around middle-class concerns—homeownership, college loans, Social Security, affordable health insurance. (I'm not saying low-income people don't need these things too, just that they are politically salient because the middle class cares about them, as it does not care, for example, about the inner city, school integration or prison reform.) John Edwards is about the only presidential candidate who mentions the 36.5 million Americans—12.3 percent—who fall below the poverty line ($10,488 for a single person, $20,444 for a family of four), and the additional 19 percent who are what sociologist Katherine Newman calls the near poor—100 to 200 percent above the poverty line. Only Edwards talks about the need to eradicate poverty, which he claims would take thirty years. So far his antipoverty platform has mostly reaped him charges of hypocrisy in the media for having a big house and getting expensive haircuts, as if there has to be something fishy about a rich man who campaigns against poverty and asks for poor people's votes. It's as if all the media talked about in 1932 was FDR's cigarette holder. A cigarette holder! Who does he think he is?

Dr. Michele's patient is lucky—she has free healthcare, and from top doctors too. What she obviously doesn't have is enough money to live on. Any emergency, and every life has them, could push her and her baby into homelessness. Significantly, affordable housing is not on the progressive agenda (affordable mortgages is something else—that's "homeownership," a middle-class shibboleth). Yet we are still facing a severe affordable-housing shortage. The rule of thumb is that a person should pay no more than 30 percent of his or her income for housing, which means that someone at the poverty level should be paying $262 a month, max. According to the 2006 Census, only 5.6 percent of New Haven's rentable housing units cost $299 per month or less. Given that 21 percent of New Havenites are below the poverty line, the vast majority of them must be doubling and tripling up, or paying far too much of their income for housing.

If Edwards has a plan to lift out of poverty Dr. Michele's patient and the millions like her, I don't care if his locks are as luxuriant as Little Lord Fauntleroy's.

Questions for 4.2

1. What does Katha Pollitt mean when she says that poverty and health are intertwined? List some of the things that illustrate this point.
2. What are some of the things that many people take for granted that are not available to people who must get by with marginal incomes?
3. Why does Pollitt call our health care system "bizarre"? What examples does she give to explain her views?
4. Why do doctors end up prescribing expensive prescription drugs to cure conditions that can be treated easily by less expensive over-the-counter medications?
5. Along with many of the other articles we looked at earlier, this article is concerned with class issues as well as poverty. What does Pollitt mean when she says that progressives now generally frame their politics around middle class issues? Why would they do that?
6. Explain the difference between middle class issues and issues that are of concern to the "near poor." For instance, what is the difference between policies designed to make affordable housing available to people versus policies that focus on making affordable mortgages a priority?
7. Pollitt's article is titled "Poverty Is Hazardous to Your Health." Discuss how persuasively she has argued for her position.

Inequality: Bad for Your Health
An Interview with Social Epidemiologist Ichiro Kawachi

Amy Gluckman and Alissa Thuotte

How do you stay healthy? That's a no brainer, right? Eat the right foods, exercise, quit smoking, get regular medical checkups. Epidemiologist *Ichiro Kawachi* wants to add a new item to the list: live in a relatively egalitarian society. *Kawachi*, a professor of social epidemiology at the Harvard School of Public Health, has carried out a wide range of research studies on the social and economic factors that account for average health outcomes in different societies. Among the most novel conclusions of this body of research is that people in societies with high levels of economic inequality are less healthy than those living in more equal societies, regardless of their absolute levels of income.

Selection 4.3

Health policy is at least on the table in this election year. The conversation, however, is almost entirely limited to whether and how to ensure universal health insurance coverage. The work of Kawachi and his colleagues suggests that the public debate about health really needs to be much broader, encompassing a wide range of public policies—in many cases economic policies—that do not explicitly address health but that nonetheless condition how long and how robust our lives will be. Their work traces the multidimensional connection between an individual's health and the qualities of her social world, many of which can shift dramatically when the gap between rich and poor widens.

Kawachi spoke with *Dollars & Sense* in November.

Dollars & Sense: Your research looks at the relationship between economic factors and health, especially whether living in a more unequal society, in itself, has a negative effect on health outcomes—and you have found evidence that it does. But I want to start by being really clear about what this hypothesis means. There seems to be such a complicated web of possible relationships between income and health.

Ichiro Kawachi: Let's start with how your own income affects your health. Most obviously, income enables people to purchase the goods and services that promote health: purchasing good, healthy food, being able to use the income to live in a safe and healthy neighborhood, being able to purchase sports equipment. Income enables people to carry out the advice of public health experts about how to behave in ways that promote longevity.

"Inequality: Bad for Your Health. An Interview with Social Epidemiologist Ichiro Kawachi," by Amy Gluckman and Alissa Thuotte, in *Dollars & Sense,* January/February 2008. Reprinted by permission of *Dollars & Sense,* a progressive economics magazine <www.dollarsandsense.org>.

But in addition to that, having a secure income has an important psychosocial effect. It provides people with a sense of control and mastery over their lives. And lots of psychologists now say that sense of control, along with the ability to plan for the future, is in itself a very important source of psychological health. Knowing that your future is secure, that you're not going to be too financially stressed, also provides incentives for people to invest in their health Put another way, if my mind is taken up with having to try to make ends meet, I don't have sufficient time to listen to my doctor's advice and invest in my health in various ways.

So there are some obvious ways in which having adequate income is important for health. This is what we call the absolute income effect—that is, the effect of your own income on your own health. If only absolute income matters, then your health is determined by your income alone, and it doesn't matter what anybody else makes. But our hypothesis has been that relative income might also matter: namely, where your income stands in relation to others'. That's where the distribution of income comes in. We have looked at the idea that when the distance between your income and the incomes of the rest of society grows very large, this may pose an additional health hazard.

D&S: How could people's relative income have an impact on health, even if their incomes are adequate in absolute terms?

IK: There are a couple of possible pathways. One is this ancient theory of relative deprivation: the idea that given a particular level of income, the greater the distance between your income and the incomes of the rest of society, the more miserable you feel. People *are* sensitive to their relative position in society vis-à-vis income. You may have a standard of living above the poverty level; nonetheless, if you live in a community or a society in which everyone else is making so much more, you might feel frustrated or miserable as a result, and this might have deleterious psychological and perhaps behavioral consequences. So that's one idea.

Another hypothesis about why income distribution matters is that when the income or wealth gap between the top and bottom grows, certain things begin to happen within the realm of politics. For example, when the wealthiest segment of society pulls away from the rest of us, they literally begin to segregate themselves in terms of where they live, and they begin to purchase services like health care and education through private means. This translates into a dynamic where wealthy people see that their tax dollars are not being spent for their own benefit, which in turn leads to a reduced basis for cooperation and spending on public goods. So I think there is an entirely separate political mechanism that's distinct from the psychological mechanism involved in notions of relative deprivation.

These are some of the key ways in which income inequality is corrosive for the public's health.

D&S: When you talk about relative deprivation, are you talking primarily about poor people, or does the evidence suggest that inequality affects health outcomes up and down the income ladder? For instance, what about the middle class? I think for the public to understand the inequality effect as something different from just the absolute-income effect, they would have to see that it isn't only poor people who can be hurt by inequality.

IK: Exactly, that's my argument. If you subscribe to the theory that it's only your own income that matters for health, then obviously middle-class people would not have much to worry about—they're able to put food on the table, they have adequate clothing and shelter, they're beyond poverty. What the relative-income theory suggests is that even middle-class people might be less healthy than they would be if they lived in a more egalitarian society.

D&S: That's what I was wondering about. Say we compared a person at the median income level in the United States versus Germany, both of whom certainly have enough income to cover all of the basic building blocks of good health. Would this hypothesis lead you to expect that, other things being equal, the middle-income person in the United States will likely have worse health because economic inequality is greater here?

IK: Yes, that's exactly right. And that's borne out. Americans are much less healthy than Europeans, for example, in spite of having higher average wealth.

D&S: But, unlike most other rich countries, the United States does not have universal health care. Couldn't that explain the poorer health outcomes here?

IK: Not entirely. There was a very interesting paper that came out last year comparing the health of Americans to the health of people in England, using very comparable, nationally representative surveys. They looked at the prevalence of major conditions such as heart attack, obesity, diabetes, hypertension. On virtually every indicator, the *top* third of Americans by income—virtually all of whom had health insurance—were still sicker than the *bottom* third of people in England. The comparison was confined to white Americans and white Britons, so they even abstracted out the contribution of racial disparities.

Health insurance certainly matters—I'm not downgrading its importance—but part of the reason Americans are so sick is because we live in a really unequal society, and it begins to tell on the physiology.

D&S: Has anyone tried to compare countries that have universal health care but have differing levels of inequality?

IK: There have been comparisons across Western European countries, all of which pretty much have universal coverage. If you compare the Scandinavian countries against the U.K. and other European countries, you generally see that the Scandinavians do have a better level of health. The more egalitarian the country, the healthier its citizens tend to be. But that's about as much as we can say. I'm not aware of really careful comparative studies; I'm making a generalization based on broad patterns.

D&S: It sounds like there is still plenty of research to do.

IK: Yes.

D&S: You have already mentioned a couple of possible mechanisms by which an unequal distribution of income could affect health. Are there any other mechanisms that you would point to?

IK: I think those are the two big ones: the political mechanism, which happens at the level of society when the income distribution widens, and then the individual mechanism, which is the relative deprivation that people feel. But I should add that relative deprivation itself can affect health through a variety of mechanisms. For instance, there is evidence that a sense of relative deprivation leads people into a spending race to try to keep up with the Joneses—a pattern of conspicuous, wasteful consumption, working in order to spend, to try to keep up with the lifestyle of the people at the top. This leads to many behaviors with deleterious health consequences, among them overwork, stress, not spending enough time with loved ones, and so forth.

Very interestingly, a couple of economists recently analyzed a study of relative deprivation, which used an index based upon the gap between your income and the incomes of everybody above you within your social comparison group, namely, people with the same occupation, or people in the same age group or living in the same state. What they found was that the greater the gap between a person's own income and the average income of their comparison group, the shorter their lives, the lower their life expectancy, as well as the higher their smoking rates, the higher their utilization of mental health services, and so on. This is suggestive evidence that deprivation relative to average income may actually matter for people's health.

D&S: It's interesting—this part of your analysis almost starts to dovetail with Juliet Schor's work.

IK: Absolutely, that's right. What Juliet Schor writes about in *The Overspent American* is consumerism. It seems to me that in a society with greater income inequality, there's so much more consumerism, that the kind of pathological behavior she describes is so much more acute in unequal societies, driven by people trying to emulate the behavior of those who are pulling away from them.

D&S: Your research no doubt reflects your background as a social epidemiologist. However, it seems as though many mainstream economists view these issues completely differently: many do not accept the existence of *any* causal effect running from income to health, except possibly to the degree that your income affects how much health care you can purchase.

IK: Yes, there is a lot of pushback from economists who, as you say, are even skeptical that absolute income matters for health. What I would say to them is, try to be a little bit open-minded about the empirical evidence. It seems to me that much of the dismissal from economists is not based upon looking at the empirical data. When they do, there is a shift: some economists are now beginning to publish studies that actually agree with what we are saying. For example, the study on relative deprivation and health I mentioned was done by a couple of economists.

Another example: some studies by an erstwhile critic of mine, Jeffrey Milyo, and Jennifer Mellor, who in the past have criticized our studies on income distribution and health in the United States as not being robust to different kinds of model specifications—a very technical debate. Anyway, most recently they published an interesting study based on an experiment in which they had participants play a prisoners' dilemma kind of game to see how much they cooperate as opposed to act selfishly. One of the things Mellor and Milyo found was that as they varied the distribution of the honoraria they paid to the participants, the more unequal the distribution of this "income," the more selfishly the players acted. They concluded that their results support what we have been contending, which is that income inequality leads to psychosocial effects where people become less trusting, less cohesive, and less likely to contribute to public spending.

D&S: That's fascinating.

IK: Yes, it's very interesting. So watch this space, because some of the recent evidence from economists themselves has begun to support what we're saying.

D&S: In other parts of the world, and especially in Africa, there are examples of societies whose economies are failing or stagnating *because of* widespread public health issues, for example HIV/AIDS. So it seems as if not only can low income cause poor health, but also that poor health can cause low income. I wonder if your research has anything to say about the complicated web between income and health that those countries are dealing with.

IK: There's no doubt that in sub-Saharan Africa, poor health is the major impediment to economic growth. You have good econometric studies suggesting that the toll of HIV, TB, and malaria alone probably slows economic growth by a measurable amount, maybe 1½ percentage points per year. So there's no question that what those countries need is investment to improve people's health, in order for them to even begin thinking about escaping the poverty trap.

The same is true in the United States, by the way. Although I've told the story in which the direction of causation runs from income to health, of course poor health is also a major cause of loss of income. When people become ill, for example, they can lose their jobs and hence their income.

What I'll say about the developing world is that in many ways, the continuing lack of improvement in health in, for example, the sub-Saharan Africa is itself an expression of the maldistribution of income in the world. As you know, the rich countries are persistently failing to meet the modest amount of funding that's being asked by the World Health Organization to solve many of these problems, like providing malaria tablets and bed nets and HIV pills for everyone in sub-Saharan Africa. If you look at inequality on a global scale, the world itself could benefit from some more redistribution. Today the top 1% of the world's population owns about a third of the world's wealth. So, although certainly the origins of the HIV epidemic are not directly related to income inequality, I think the solution lies in redistributing wealth and income through overseas development aid, from the 5% of the world who live in the rich countries to everyone else.

D&S: Leaving aside some of the countries with the most devastating public health problems, poor countries in general are often focused just on economic growth, on getting their per capita GDP up, but this often means that inequality increases as well—like in China. Do you view the inequality effect as significant enough that a developing country concerned about its health outcomes should aim to limit the growth of inequality even if that meant sacrificing some economic growth?

IK: It depends on the country's objectives. But I'd ask the question: what is the purpose of economic growth if not to assure people's level of well-being, which includes their health? Why do people care about economic growth? In order to lead a satisfying and long life, many people would say. If that's the case, then many people living in developing countries may feel exactly as you suggest: they would prefer policies that attend to egalitarian distribution over policies that are aimed purely at growth.

Amartya Sen has written about this; he has pointed to many countries that are poor but nonetheless enjoy a very good level of health. He cites examples like Costa Rica and the Kerala region in India, which are much, much poorer than the United States but enjoy a high level of health. It really depends on the objectives of the country's politicians. In Kerala and Costa Rica, their health record is very much a reflection of how their governments have invested their income in areas that promote health, like education and basic health services—even if doing so means causing a bit of a drag on economic growth.

China also had this record until perhaps ten years ago. Now they're in this era of maximizing growth, and we're seeing a very steep rise in inequality. Although we don't have good health statistics from China, my guess is that this is probably going to tell on its national health status. Actually, we already know that improvement in their child mortality rates for children under five has begun to slow down in the last 20 years, since the introduction of their economic reforms. In the 1950s and 1960s, the records seemed to suggest quite rapid improvements in health in China. But that's begun to slow down.

D&S: Certainly your research on the health effects of inequality could represent a real challenge in the United States in terms of health care policy. In many ways we have a very advanced health care system, but many people are not well served by it. What effect do you think your work could or should have on U.S. health policy?

IK: Regardless of whether you believe what I'm saying about income inequality, the most basic interpretation of this research is that there are many things that determine people's health besides simply access to good health services. We spend a lot of time discussing how to improve health insurance coverage in this country. In the current presidential debates, when they talk about health policy, they're mostly talking about health insurance. But it's myopic to confine discussions of health policy to what's going to be done about health insurance. There are many social determinants of health and thus many other policy options for improving Americans' health. Investing in education, reducing the disparities in income, attacking problems of poverty, improving housing for poor people, investing in neighborhood services and amenities—these are all actually health policies. The most fundamental point about this whole area of research is that there are many determinants of health besides what the politicians call health policy.

D&S: Besides doctors and medical care.

IK: Yes, that's right. I used to be a physician, and physicians do a lot of good, but much of health is also shaped by what goes on outside the health care system. That's probably the most important thing.

The second thing is the implication that income certainly matters for health. So policies that affect peoples' incomes, both absolute and relative income, may have health consequences. For instance, I think the kinds of tax policies we have had in recent years—where most of the benefits have accrued to the top 1% and the resulting budget deficits have led to cutbacks of services to the rest of us, especially those in the bottom half of the income distribution—have been a net negative for public health, through the kind of political mechanism I have described.

D&S: It's almost as though there should be a line for health care in the cost-benefit analysis of any change in tax policies or other economic policies.

IK: Absolutely. There's an idea in public health called the health impact assessment. It's a technique modeled after environmental impact assessments, a set of tools that people are advocating should be used at the Cabinet level. The idea is that when, say, the treasury secretary suggests some new economic measure, then we can formally put the proposal through a modeling exercise to forecast its likely effects on health. Health certainly is very sensitive to decisions that are made elsewhere in the Cabinet besides what goes on in Health and Human Services.

D&S: What about global health policy? Are groups like the World Health Organization paying attention to the kind of research that you do?

IK: Yes, they are. Maybe seven or eight years ago, the WHO had a commission on macroeconomics and health, headed by Jeffrey Sachs. The idea was, by increasing funding to tackle big health problems in the developing world, we can also improve their economic performance and end poverty. That commission posed the direction of causality from health to income. In the last three years, the WHO has had a new commission on the social determinants of health, headed by a social epidemiologist from England, Michael Marmot. That group is looking at the other direction of causality—namely, from poverty to ill health—and considering the ways in which government policies in different areas can improve people's social environment in order to improve their health. I think they are due to report next year with some recommendations as well as case examples from different countries, mostly developing countries whose governments have tried to tackle the economic side of things in order to improve health outcomes.

D&S: Right now the United States is continuing on this path of becoming more and more economically stratified. Your work suggests that that doesn't bode well for us in terms of health. I wonder—this is very speculative—but if we stay on this path of worsening inequality, what do you predict our health as a country is likely to look like in 20 or 30 years?

IK: We're already in the bottom third of the 23 OECD countries, the rich countries, in terms of our average health status. Most people are dimly aware that we spend over half of the medical dollars expended on this planet, so they assume that we should therefore be able to purchase the highest level of health. I teach a course on social determinants of health at Harvard, and many of my students are astonished to discover that America is not number one in life expectancy.

I predict that if we continue on this course of growing income inequality, we will continue to slip further. That gains in life expectancy will continue to slow down. Life expectancy is increasing every year, probably because of medical advances, but I suspect that eventually there will be a limit to how much can be delivered through high-tech care and that our health will slip both in relative terms, compared to the rest of the OECD countries, and maybe even in absolute terms, losing some of the gains we have had over the last half century. For example, some demographers are already forecasting that life expectancy will drop in the coming century because of the obesity epidemic. Add that to the possible effects of income inequality, and I could easily imagine a scenario in which life expectancy might decline in absolute terms as well as in relative terms. It's likely that we have not yet seen the full impact of the recent rise in inequality on health status, because it takes a while for the full health effects to become apparent in the population.

Questions for 4.3

1. Why does Dr. Kawachi maintain that focusing on whether and how to ensure universal coverage is too limited?
2. What important issues are we encouraged to ignore by focusing exclusively on universal coverage?
3. What are some concrete examples of how having adequate income affects health?
4. What is meant by the distinction between absolute income and relative income?
5. Explain the effects of relative deprivation on peoples' health.
6. What are the psychosocial effects of income inequality?
7. Has Kawachi persuaded you that a more egalitarian society is in everyone's interests? Explain your answer.

Crime and Punishment

The first article in Chapter 5 is a good example of what is often called "blaming the victim." You might want to take another look at the description of "blaming the victim" in the Introduction to this book to prepare yourself for tackling this chapter.

Written about crime and punishment from the narrow perspective of a black prosecutor in Louisville, Kentucky, Felcicia Nu'Man focuses on individual criminal behavior. The prosecutor tells us that she was hired not to be a social worker but to enforce the law, and she tries to defend herself against the charge, implicit or explicit, that she is carrying out the directions of a racist criminal justice system. Although she acknowledges that black people are treated unfairly, she is incapable or unwilling to integrate her understanding of the systemic nature of racial and economic inequality with a critique of the system as a whole and the context in which punishments of crimes are meted out by the criminal justice system.

In sharp contrast to the Nu'Man article, the other two articles ask us to think about the problems of crime and punishment in the social context of who gets arrested and prosecuted. They demonstrate what it means to use the lenses of race and class to frame or define the problem and come up with appropriate solutions. Both of these articles provide good illustrations of the right way and the wrong way to think about the problem of crime and punishment and the criminal justice system The article by Erik Eckholm of the *New York Times* examines the racial gap in drug arrests, and the article by Ellis Cose explores the harm of "get tough" policies. One approach to framing the problem takes notice of the unequal treatment that is built into the criminal justice system and that must be acknowledged and addressed if we are to have any hope of solving the problem. Nu'Man's article fails to recognize racial and economic inequality, and thus the "solution" the writer proposes is more about reinforcing the status quo than adopting policies designed to bring us closer to equality. If you solve the wrong problem, you may have the illusion of success but be perpetuating rather than dismantling the inequities built into the system.

Further Reading

Associated Press. "Sentences Reduced for 3000 Cocaine Inmates." *New York Times,* April 25, 2008.

Saunders, Debra J. "Drug Laws' Absence of Justice." *San Francisco Chronicle,* March 6, 2008.

Stemen, Don. *Crime and Incarceration.* Vera Institute, 2007.

I Am Not the Enemy

Felicia J. Nu'Man

I put people in jail because they break the law, not because I'm a puppet of a racist judicial system.

I battle crime every day, and I defend myself every day, too. I'm a black prosecutor in Louisville, Ky. I have presented cases before juries, but from my first day on the job I have felt that I have been on trial in the court of public opinion. Even my maternal grandmother once asked if I was a Republican (I'm not), while others just asked the ultimate question: how can you put our black men in jail?

Depending on my mood, the answer can be a three-part speech on the decay of moral values, educational-attainment

Selection 5.1

levels and teenage motherhood. Other times I simply tell them the defendants put themselves in the penitentiary and I facilitated their exodus from the community. Or better yet, my favorite answer: I didn't put the crack in their pocket and a gun in the other.

It's difficult to combat the impression that somehow I am personally persecuting these men and not performing a public function of law enforcement. I have no problem sending a drug dealer or a drug user to jail. I know that I'm doing important work to keep the streets safe, not just from drugs but from the virus of the drug culture. The virus of criminality. The virus of fast money at all costs. The virus of adrenaline addiction. The virus of chaos addiction.

A friend once said that drug dealers need a 12-step program to recover from the lifestyles they lead. Young men filled with testosterone and bravado don't mix well with little guidance and the lure of quick money. Hundreds or thousands of dollars of disposable income made in a few hours is a difficult life to reject when all that is offered as an alternative is a minimum-wage job. When your mother is addicted to drugs or her lost childhood, and your father is absent, you start life with a cinder block around your neck. Young males notoriously make bad decisions. But these bad decisions are deadly.

My job is not that of a social worker or a social scientist. I was hired to enforce the laws as drafted. I have a duty to the citizens of the Commonwealth of Kentucky, including all the black victims of the drug culture. These victims are not just the dead rival drug dealers but the addicted mothers who

"I Am Not the Enemy," by Felicia Nu'Man, from *Newsweek,* April 14, 2008. Reprinted with the permission of the author, Felicia Nu'Man.

neglect their children, the neglected children themselves and the overburdened extended families who care for these addicts and their children.

Many surreptitiously accuse me of being a race traitor, a puppet of a racist criminal-justice system. Race does not enter the equation for me. My question to these black people who believe me to be a traitor is, when will you connect the dots? Please realize, the police and the prosecutors are not the problem; it is the criminals in these depressed neighborhoods who are. These young, directionless men are the true menace. In order to settle the score, many think protection for these "victims" can be had through jury nullification, impeding investigations and elevating "social"-justice instigators who demonize all police. There are prosecutors and police who are not pure of heart and definitely have an agenda, hidden or obvious. But how do these young men find themselves in the criminal-justice system? Their choices. In the past, black people argued for justice from a place of moral superiority, but now who can take seriously anyone who defends drug dealers, child abusers, wife beaters or rapists? The victims deserve more.

In my county, two thirds of all the criminal defendants are black, which means that roughly two thirds of all victims are black. Should law enforcement not prosecute black criminals and doom all black victims to the absence of justice? Why aren't the police and the prosecutor seen as the champions of the black victim? There is a disconnect in the mind of many black people. My great-grandfather was murdered in Kentucky back in the 1940s. There was no investigation. There was no prosecution of the people involved. There was only a funeral, a widow and fatherless children. This would never happen today. Criminal acts—violent or otherwise—will not be tolerated by any person regardless of race. The system is not perfect, but have you seen the alternatives out there? We have the most perfect imperfect system on earth.

Of course, it's harder to be black in this country. Of course, black people are treated unfairly. Of course, the inner cities have a decaying infrastructure. But there is absolutely no reason to break a reasonable, appropriate law. None. The alternative is chaos.

Questions for 5.1

1. Is it helpful to frame the conversation in terms of who is "the enemy"?
2. What are the implications of framing the question in this way?
3. Why does Nu'Man say, "Race does not enter the equation for me . . ."?
4. Nu'Man maintains that neither the police nor the prosecutors nor the "racist criminal justice system" is the problem. Who or what according to Nu'man is the problem? Do you agree?

5. Nu'man seems to focus almost exclusively on the fact of law-breaking without examining the broader issues in which the criminal justice system identifies and prosecutes individuals. What is gained and what is lost by framing the question so narrowly?

6. In the final paragraph of this piece, Nu'man acknowledges that "of course, black people are treated unfairly" and recognizes that "the inner cities have decaying infrastructures," but she doesn't seem to address these mitigating factors. How would you explain some of the obvious contradictions or inconsistencies in this piece?

7. What is the rationale for "punishment" and what should be its goal?

Reports Find Racial Gap in Drug Arrests

Erik Eckholm

More than two decades after President Ronald Reagan escalated the war on drugs, arrests for drug sales or, more often, drug possession are still rising. And despite public debate and limited efforts to reduce them, large disparities persist in the rate at which blacks and whites are arrested and imprisoned for drug offenses, even though the two races use illegal drugs at roughly equal rates.

Two new reports, issued Monday by the Sentencing Project in Washington and by Human Rights Watch in New York, both say the racial disparities reflect, in large part, an overwhelming focus of law enforcement on drug use in low-income urban areas, with arrests and incarceration the main weapon.

Selection 5.2

But they note that the murderous crack-related urban violence of the 1980s, which spawned the war on drugs, has largely subsided, reducing the rationale for a strategy that has sowed mistrust in the justice system among many blacks.

In 2006, according to federal data, drug-related arrests climbed to 1.89 million, up from 1.85 million in 2005 and 581,000 in 1980.

More than four in five of the arrests were for possession of banned substances, rather than for their sale or manufacture. Four in 10 of all drug arrests were for marijuana possession, according to the latest F.B.I. data.

Apart from crowding prisons, one result is a devastating impact on the lives of black men: they are nearly 12 times as likely to be imprisoned for drug convictions as adult white men, according to the Human Rights Watch report.

Others are arrested for possession of small quantities of drugs and later released, but with a permanent blot on their records anyway.

"The way the war on drugs has been pursued is one of the biggest reasons for the growing racial disparities in criminal justice over all," said Ryan S. King, a policy analyst with the Sentencing Project who wrote its report, which focuses on the differential in arrest rates, not only between races but also among cities around the country. Some cities pursue urban, minority drug use far more intensively than do others.

Both Democratic presidential candidates, Senator Barack Obama of Illinois and Senator Hillary Rodham Clinton of New York, have strongly condemned the racial disparities in arrests and incarceration during their campaigns, although neither has said how they would end them.

Two-thirds of those arrested for drug violations in 2006 were white and 33 percent were black, although blacks made up 12.8 percent of the population, F.B.I. data show. National data are not collected on ethnicity, and arrests of Hispanics may be in either category.

"The race question is so entangled in the way the drug war was conceived," said Jamie Fellner, a senior counsel at Human Rights Watch and the author of its report.

"If the drug issue is still seen as primarily a problem of the black inner city, then we'll continue to see this enormously disparate impact," Ms. Fellner said.

Her report cites federal data from 2003, the most recent available on this aspect, indicating that blacks constituted 53.5 percent of all who entered prison for a drug conviction.

Some crime experts say that the disparities exist for sound reasons. Heather Mac Donald, a fellow at the Manhattan Institute in New York, said it made sense for police to focus more on fighting visible drug dealing in low-income urban areas, largely involving members of minorities, than on hidden use in suburban homes, more often by whites, because the urban street trade is more associated with violence and other crimes and impairs the quality of life.

"The disparities reflect policing decisions to use drug laws to try and reduce violence and to respond to the demand by law-abiding residents in poor neighborhoods to clean up the drug trade," Ms. Mac Donald said.

But what people in low-income urban areas need is not more incarceration but improved public safety, Mr. King said. "Arresting hundreds of thousands of young African-American men hasn't ended street-corner drug sales."

A shift of resources toward drug treatment and social services rather than wholesale incarceration, he said, would do more to improve conditions in blighted neighborhoods.

Limited efforts have been made to shift policies in ways that may reduce racial differences. Many states are experimenting with so-called drug courts, which send users to treatment rather than prison. This does not, however, affect arrest rates, which have lifelong consequences even for those who are never convicted or imprisoned.

Police in a few cities including Denver, Seattle and Oakland, Calif., have said they are spending fewer resources on arrests for lower-lever offenses like marijuana possession.

In December, the United States Sentencing Commission amended the federal sentencing guidelines for convictions involving crack cocaine, which is more often used by blacks, somewhat reducing the length of sentences compared with those for convictions involving powder cocaine. But mandatory and longer sentences for crack violations remain embedded in federal and state laws.

Questions for 5.2

1. What is the problem on which this article focuses?
2. According to this article, how are issues of race and the drug war intertwined? Be specific.
3. How does the author explain the large disparities in the rate at which blacks and whites are arrested and imprisoned for drug offenses even though the two races use illegal drugs at roughly equal rates?
4. According to a recent Human Rights Watch report, black males are nearly 12 times as likely to be imprisoned for drug convictions as adult white men. What long-term impact does this fact have on the lives of black men?
5. What, according to this article, would improve conditions in low-income urban neighborhoods?
6. How does the way in which the problem is defined lead to different "solutions?

The Harm of "Get Tough" Policies

Ellis Cose

The Supreme Court's ruling on federal cocaine sentences could be a turning point—toward justice and righting an old wrong.

For two decades, the federal government has pursued, prosecuted and sentenced cocaine offenders in a way that borders on insanity—targeting petty criminals over serious drug dealers—while fostering contempt, instead of respect, for the policies that have sent tens of thousands to jail. On Monday, the Supreme Court said enough was enough and empowered federal judges to reject sentencing guidelines rooted in hysteria and ignorance. The move has considerable support on the federal bench. It allows judges "who actually see the people and understand the local community" to better consider their communities' best interests, said Jack B. Weinstein, a federal district judge in New York.

The significance of the issue—and the enormity of the shift in expert opinion—was underscored a day later. The U.S. Sentencing Commission took the unprecedented step of announcing, unanimously, that nearly 20,000 federal inmates convicted of crack possession could apply for (relatively small) reductions in sentences. "In this business, you don't get too many good days . . . Now, two in a row," said Marc Mauer of the Sentencing Project, a Washington-based organization that tracks criminal-justice trends.

The court's two 7–2 decisions—authored by Ruth Bader Ginsburg and John Paul Stevens, respectively—contained no rousing rhetoric; they methodically built on the logic of two prior opinions. But Ginsburg's ruling catalogued, at length, criticisms of federal cocaine policy. "This may be the first sentencing decision since the mid 1980s that actually talks about justice, that seems to have some blood in it," said Graham Boyd, director of the ACLU's drug law reform project. Boyd compared the potential impact of Ginsburg's decision to the famous *Brown v. Board of Education* desegregation ruling. "When the Supreme Court says that something is wrong, the other institutions of government pay attention," said Boyd.

Ginsburg's carefully worded decision did not exactly say the Feds were wrong, but it explicitly gave federal judges permission to reach that conclusion on their own. The case revolved around a former Marine who had fought in

Desert Storm and had no prior convictions and a good work record. Police found Derrick Kimbrough and a companion in a car with crack, powder cocaine and a gun. Kimbrough's guilty plea to four felonies should have sent him to prison for at least 19 years. The trial judge noted that had Kimbrough possessed powder cocaine in the same quantity as the combination of powder and crack, his potential prison time would have been more than halved. Judge Raymond Jackson split the difference, sentencing Kimbrough to 15 years. The appeals court said he was out of line; the Supreme Court ruled he was not.

On its face, the debate was over how much deference had to be paid to the guidelines; but it was also over whether those guidelines made sense. For embodied in them was the notion that a defendant caught with 50 grams of crack should face the same penalty as one with 5,000 grams of powder cocaine. Yet, crack is nothing more than powder cocaine and baking soda dissolved in water that is boiled away. And, as Ginsburg pointed out, they "have the same physiological and psychotropic effects." So why is possession treated so differently?

The answer lies in the Anti-Drug Abuse Act of 1986. In crafting the law, Congress concluded that someone dealing a small quantity of crack was the functional equivalent of someone dealing a large quantity of powder. Why conclude such a strange thing? Eric Sterling, then assistant counsel to the House Committee on the Judiciary, fingers an "expert consultant" named Jehru St. Valentine Brown. A narcotics detective when not advising Congress, Brown convinced legislators that "a trafficker in 20 grams of crack cocaine was trafficking at the same 'serious' level . . . as a trafficker in 1,000 grams of powder cocaine," said Sterling. Given such expert advice, it made sense to treat the drugs very differently—all the more so given the widespread conviction that crack was a superaddictive drug, spawning crack babies and rampant violence on a scale society had never before encountered. Fear took the place of science, leading the sentencing commission to adopt and build upon the 100-to-1 scheme embodied in the statute.

The result has been a tragic playing out of the law of unintended consequences. Instead of focusing on dangerous drug kingpins, federal efforts have been mostly directed at people possessing relatively small amounts of crack. Only 7 percent of federal cocaine cases are directed at high-level traffickers, with a third of all cases involving quantities that weigh less than a small candy bar, says Sterling, who now runs the Criminal Justice Policy Foundation: "Street-level crack dealers are actually punished 300 times more severely than high-level cocaine powder traffickers on a punishment-per-gram basis." To add to the mess, drug policy has become highly racialized. As Ginsberg noted, approximately 85 percent of those convicted of crack offenses in federal court are black—even though more whites than blacks use crack. The numbers, says Sterling, reflect "conventions of law enforcement" and a predisposition toward "prosecuting a class of lowlifes who happen to be people of color."

Whether this is indeed a watershed moment is yet to be seen. Even the Supreme Court's influence is limited. In the end, "all the courts do is interpret the law," said Deborah Small of Break the Chains, a New York nonprofit promoting drug-policy reform. But Judge Weinstein is among those who believe things are changing. "There is a sense of a turning point," he told *Newsweek.* "And partly it's due to economics. The cost [of the current path] is tremendous, to the community and to taxpayers."

For more than a decade, the sentencing commission has been urging Congress to rethink the law and its crack-powder ratio to no avail. This year, the commission took matters in its own hands and slightly reduced the sentencing disparity. And it again appealed to Congress to change the underlying law. The message is simple: it's not just that the "get tough" policies of the 1980s don't work; they actually do harm—by, among other things, undermining faith in the fairness and efficacy of the justice system itself. The Supreme Court finally has noticed that. It's time that Congress did the same.

Questions for 5.3

1. What has been the effect of the way the United States has prosecuted and sentenced cocaine offenders over the past two decades?
2. Explain the different ways that powder and crack cocaine have been treated by the law. Why has it been the case that someone caught with 50 grams of crack and someone caught with 5,000 grams of powder were treated the same way?
3. What have been the unintended consequences of the way penalties have been determined for crack versus powder cocaine?
4. What problem are "get tough" policies designed to address?
5. According to this article, how do the "get tough" policies do harm to the judicial system?

Abstinence: Whose Privilege, Whose Power?

Purity balls? Virginity pledges? Promise rings? Or as a recent article in *The New Yorker* asked, "Why do so many evangelical teenagers become pregnant?" The three articles in Chapter 6 ask you to think about the current preoccupation with issues of sexuality and the place of sex in our lives. The first article, written by feminist writer and columnist Jennifer Baumgardner, asks, "Would you pledge your virginity to your father?" This question arises in the context of "abstinence only" education, which was funded by the Bush administration. Baumgardner reports: "In 1996, after lobbying by the religious right, Congress allocated nearly half a billion dollars for public schools nationwide to adopt sex ed programs that advocate abstinence-only education." This article, as well as the one that follows by Margaret Talbot, explores the impact of imposing "abstinence only" on the sexual activity (or lack of it) of young people at different ages and of different religions, in different parts of the country, of different social and economic backgrounds and other factors as well. The results are both fascinating and disturbing.

The final article in Chapter 6 takes the gloves off and speaks its mind: Katha Pollitt asks, "Is the Pope Crazy?" She was first moved to ask that question in the fall of 2003 in response to public statements by Pope John Paul II. In a column in *The Nation* that year, she argued: "It's bad enough to argue that condoms are against God's will while millions die [of STDs]. But to maintain, falsely, that they are ineffective in order to discourage their use is truly immoral. If not insane." More recently, in March of 2009 on a visit to Yaounde, Pope Benedict said of the AIDS pandemic, "You can't resolve it with the distribution of condoms. On the contrary, it increases the problem."

Rebecca Hodes of the Treatment Action Campaign in South Africa said that if the pope is serious about preventing HIV infections, he should focus on promoting wide access to condoms and spreading information on how to use them. Who has the better answer to "What's the Problem?" and who proposes the best solution? Underlying all three pieces is a question about whose interests are served by the way we teach about and talk about sex and sexuality. Whose privilege? Whose power?

Further Reading

Dailard, Cynthia. "Understanding 'Abstinence'": Implications for Individuals, Programs, and Policies." *Guttmacher Report on Public Policy* 6 (5: December 2003).

Fort, Sarah. "Fatal Error: Bush's Global AIDS Plan Ignores Reality and Endangers Women's Health." *Ms.* magazine, msmagazine.com/fall2006.

"Government Report Shows that Abstinence Ed Doesn't Work." *Ms.* magazine, msmagazine.com, 2008.

Larson, Krista, and Enanueal Tumanjong. "Pope Says Condoms Won't Solve AIDS." Associated Press, March 2009.

Would You Pledge Your Virginity to Your Father?

Jennifer Baumgardner

It's like a wedding but with a twist: Young women exchange rings, take vows and enjoy a first dance . . . with their dads. "Purity balls" are the next big thing in the save-it-till-marriage movement. Smart or scary?

In a chandelier-lit ballroom overlooking the Rocky Mountains one recent evening, some hundred couples feast on herb-crusted chicken and julienned vegetables. The men look dapper in tuxedos; their dates are resplendent in floor-length gowns, long white gloves and tiaras framing twirly, ornate updos. Seated at a table with four couples, I watch as the gray-haired man next to me reaches into his breast pocket, pulls out a small satin box and flips it open to check out a gold ring he's about to place on the finger of the woman sitting to his right. Her eyes well up with tears as she is overcome by emotion.

The man's date? His 25-year-old daughter. Welcome to Colorado Springs' Seventh Annual Father-Daughter Purity Ball, held at the five-star Broadmoor Hotel. The event's purpose is, in part, to celebrate dad-daughter bonding, but the main agenda is for fathers to vow to protect the girls' chastity until they marry and for the daughters to promise to stay pure. Pastor Randy Wilson, host of the event and cofounder of the ball, strides to the front of the room, takes the microphone and asks the men, "Are you ready to war for your daughters' purity?"

Wilson's voice is jovial, yet his message is serious—and spreading like wildfire. Dozens of these lavish events are held every year, mainly in the South and Midwest, from Tucson to Peoria and New Orleans, sponsored by churches, nonprofit groups and crisis pregnancy centers. The balls are all part of the evangelical Christian movement, and they embody one of its key doctrines: abstinence until marriage. Thousands of girls have taken purity vows at these events over the past nine years. While the abstinence movement itself is fairly mainstream—about 10 percent of teen boys and 16 percent of girls in the United States have signed virginity pledges at churches, rallies or programs sponsored by groups such as True Love Waits—purity balls represent its more extreme edge. The young women who sign covenants at these parties tend to be devout, homeschooled and sheltered from popular culture.

Randy Wilson's 19-year-old, Khrystian, is typical: She works at her church, spends most weekends at home with her family and has never danced with a male other than her father or brother. Emily Smith, an 18-year-old I meet, says that even kissing is out for her. "I made a promise to myself when I was younger," she says, "to save my first kiss for my wedding day." A tenet of the abstinence movement is that having lovers before marriage often leads to divorce. In the Wilsons' community, young women hope to meet suitors at church, at college or through family connections.

The majority of the girls here are, as purity ball guidelines suggest, "just old enough . . . [to] have begun menstruating." But a couple dozen fathers have also brought girls under 10. "This evening is more about spending time with her than her purity at this point," says one seven-year-old's dad, a trifle sheepishly. The event is seemingly innocent—not once do I hear "sex" or "virgin" cross anyone's lips. Still, every one of the girls here, even the four-year-old, will sign that purity covenant.

Encouraging girls to avoid sleeping around is, without a doubt, a good thing. The same goes for dad-daughter bonding; research shows that girls who have solid relationships with their fathers are more likely to grow up to be confident, self-respecting, successful women and to make wise choices along the way. Question is, is putting girls' purity on a pedestal the way to achieve these all-important goals?

Fathers who are protective of their daughters' virginity are nothing new. "Keep your flower safe!" a good friend's dad used to tell her when we were in college, and we'd laugh—both because it was too late for her virginity and because there was something distasteful to us about his trying to control her sex life. Recently, though, protecting girls' virginity has become a national, not just familial, concern. In 1996, after lobbying by the religious right, Congress allocated nearly half a billion dollars for public schools nationwide to adopt sex ed programs that advocate abstinence only. Today, all but a few states use government money for classes that basically warn against any sexual activity outside of marriage.

The movement's latest mission is to make abstinence cool (it's been called "chastity chic"). There are Christian rock concerts where attendees sign pledges, [Web] sites like geocities.com/thevirginclub that list stars who have held off on sex until marriage (Jessica Simpson, divorce notwithstanding, is one of their patron saints), and supportive bloggers (abstinence.net features one called "The Professional Virgin"). Silver Ring Thing, a national abstinence group for teens, has an active MySpace page filled with comments like this from "Brianna": "I vowed to stay a virgin till marriage two years ago and it's been a long tough road . . . but it gets a lil' easier everyday."

The first purity ball, with all its queen-for-a-day allure, was thrown in 1998 by Wilson, now 48, and his wife, Lisa, 47; the two run Generations of Light, a popular Christian ministry in Colorado Springs. "We wanted to set a standard of dignity and honor for the way the girls should be treated by the men in their lives," says Lisa, a warm, exuberant woman with a ready smile and seven children, ages 4 to 22. Lisa's own father left her family when she was two, and despite a kind stepfather, she says, she grew up not feeling valued or understood. "Looking back, it's a miracle I remained pure," she says. "I believe if girls feel beautiful and cherished by their fathers, they don't go looking for love from random guys."

That first ball got some positive local and Christian press, as well as inquiries from people in 21 states interested in throwing their own. Today, South Dakota's Abstinence Clearinghouse—a major association of the purity movement—sends out about 700 "Purity Ball Planner" booklets a year (tips include printing out the vows on "beautiful paper" and serving wedding cake for dessert). While the Wilsons make no money from their ball, a cottage industry for accessories has sprung up. Roam the Internet and you'll find a $250 14-karat pearl-and-diamond purity ring; for $15, you can buy a red baby-doll T-shirt with "I'm Waiting" emblazoned on the chest, its snug fit sending a bit of a mixed message.

The older girls at the Broadmoor tonight are themselves curvaceous and sexy in backless dresses and artful makeup; next to their fathers, some look disconcertingly like wives. In fact, in the parlance of the purity ball folks, one-on-one time with dad is a "date," and the only sanctioned one a girl can have until she is "courted" by a man. The roles are clear: Dad is the only man in a girl's life until her husband arrives, a lifestyle straight out of biblical times. "In patriarchy, a father owns a girl's sexuality," notes psychologist and feminist author Carol Gilligan, Ph.D. "And like any other property, he guards it, protects it, even loves it."

When it's time for dads and daughters to take the pledge (some informally exchange rings as well), the men stand over their seated daughters and read aloud from parchment imprinted with the covenant: "I, [father's name], choose before God to cover my daughter as her authority and protection in the area of purity. . . . " The men inscribe their names and their daughters sign as witnesses. Then everyone returns to their meals and an excited buzz fills the room.

Purity balls are, in fact, part of a larger trend throughout American culture of fathers spending more time with their daughters and sons—the amount rose from 2.6 hours a week in 1965 to 6.5 hours in 2000, the most recent year for which statistics are available. This togetherness has a real pay-off for girls: Those who are close with their fathers generally do better in life than those who aren't. Dan Kindlon, Ph.D., a Harvard-based psychologist who did in-depth interviews with 113 girls and teens for his new book, Alpha Girls, found that those who had the best relationships with their dads were the most accomplished academically and had the strongest sense of self. Another much-cited study on the subject by two sociologists tracked 126 Baltimore girls from low-income families. It found that those with involved and caring dads were twice as likely to go to college or find a stable job after high school than those without such fathers; 75 percent less likely to give birth as teens; 80 percent less likely to ever be in jail; and half as likely to experience significant depression.

Of course, adolescence poses a tricky challenge: Teens are often more interested in hanging out with friends than in spending time with dear old Dad. And their fathers may not be sure how to treat a child who's morphing into a young woman. (I vividly recall the betrayed look my father gave me when he caught me, at 14, emerging from a makeout session in my room.) Some experts wonder if dads' involvement in the family is seeming less important these days, given mothers' more dominant role—they're becoming the breadwinners in record numbers. Says Margo Maine, Ph.D., a clinical psychologist in West Hartford, Connecticut, who often works with families, "Our culture—and even fathers themselves—underestimates the power fathers have on women's self-esteem and identity."

Randy Wilson wants to change that. With his bright smile, steady eye contact and the erect posture of a small but confident man, he reminds me of the magnetic self-help guru that Tom Cruise portrayed in Magnolia. "Way to go, men!" Wilson says. "I applaud your courage to look your daughter in the eye and tell her how beautiful she is. If you haven't done it yet, I'll give you a chance to do it right now."

I strike up a conversation with Christy Parcha, an 18-year-old brunette who's here to perform a ballet later on; her 10-year-old sister is attending the ball with their dad, Mike, a math teacher at a local community college. Christy's eyes are bright, her cheeks flushed, and a smile permanently animates her face. Although she just graduated from high school, she is not going to college but instead will be teaching ballet classes, continuing with piano lessons and writing a book about "emotional purity," which Christy thinks is even more important than the physical kind. "I am just trying to reserve all those special feelings for my husband," she says ardently.

As it turns out, not allowing herself to think sexual thoughts makes her nervous, too, because she wants to experience pleasure with her future husband: "I don't want to be a burden to him in that I am not enjoying [sex]." Recently, a friend took her to see a movie about Queen Esther, *One Night with the King*—"a really romantic story," according to Christy. "So I watched it and I had these huge feelings rise up inside me, and I was like, 'OK, they are still there!'" she says, flopping back in her chair with relief. Still, Christy doesn't want to date. She associates sex outside of marriage as a girl "getting used, betrayed, having guys deceive you, all that kind of thing."

Other girls at the ball are far less eloquent about the pledge they've just made. To them, the excitement of the ball is buying fancy dresses and primping; one 14-year-old in the bathroom tells me she started getting ready at 9 A.M. When I ask Hannah Smith, 15, what purity means to her, she answers, "I actually don't know." Her older sister Emily jumps in: "Purity, it means . . . I don't know how to explain it. It is important to us that we promise to ourselves and to our fathers and to God that we promise to stay pure until . . . It is hard to explain." I suspect that the girls' lack of vocabulary has to do with a universal truth of girlhood: You don't want to talk about sex with anyone older than 18, particularly your dad. At the same time, the girls seem so unsure of the reasons behind their vows that I can't help but wonder if they've just signed a contract whose terms they didn't fully understand.

There is no data on whether girls who attend purity balls remain abstinent until marriage; chances are many do, given the tight-knit communities they live in. But there is striking evidence that more than half of teens who take virginity pledges—at, say, rallies or events—go on to have sex within three years, according to findings of the National Longitudinal Study of Adolescent Health, the most comprehensive survey of teens ever taken. And 88 percent of the pledgers surveyed end up having sex before marriage. "No pledge can counter the fact that teenagers are, in fact, sexual beings postpuberty," notes Cary Backenger, a clinical psychotherapist in Appleton, Wisconsin, who works with teens, including several who have taken virginity pledges. "You can't turn that off."

Disturbingly, the adolescent health study also found that STD rates were significantly higher in communities with a high proportion of pledgers. "Pledgers are less likely than nonpledgers to use condoms, so if they do have sex it is less safe," says Peter Bearman, Ph.D., a Columbia University sociologist who helped design the study. For these teens, he believes, it's a mind game: If you have condoms, you were planning to have sex. If you don't, sex wasn't premeditated, which makes it more OK. The study also found that even pledgers who remained virgins were highly likely to have oral and anal sex—risky behavior given that most probably didn't use condoms to cut their risk.

Curiously, the teen pregnancy rate is on the decline nationwide. Proponents of an abstinence-only philosophy point to this as evidence that pledges work. But a just-released study by the Mailman School of Public Health at Columbia University attributed 14 percent of this drop to teens holding off on sex—and 86 percent to teens using more effective forms of birth control, like the Pill. Says study author John Santelli, M.D., a specialist in adolescent medicine, "If most of the progress in reducing teen pregnancy rates is due to improved contraceptive use, national policy needs to catch up with those realities."

Leaders of the abstinence movement firmly believe, however, that teaching kids about the mechanics of sex and contraception "arouses" them, sparking them to have sex. They claim that those who break their vows were not "strong" pledgers to begin with, and that many more teens do keep them (teens the researchers didn't speak to). "Kids who abstain are not out there breaking hearts; they're not dogs in heat. They go on to have great, intimate sex," says Leslee Unruh, president of the Abstinence Clearinghouse. "The purity movement celebrates sex but not sex outside of commitment."

Girls who are getting married do need information about sex, Unruh continues, and she's there to provide it. (On one occasion, "I had a girl call me from her wedding," she says.) "I let them know what to expect, that there might be some discomfort," and she gives detailed information about touching and lubricants when necessary. Unruh thinks purity balls are a commendable way to get girls who want to stay virgins to do so. As she says, "They help girls realize that their fathers care deeply about their future, and then they decide to keep themselves pure."

Many experts strongly disagree. "Virginity pledges set girls up for failure," contends Kindlon, who specializes in adolescent behavior. "I like the father-daughter bonding part of the balls, but it is unfortunate that it is around a pledge that is doomed. I always counsel parents to try to encourage teens to delay sex. But when you completely forbid teens to be sexual, it can do them more harm than good. It's like telling kids not to eat candy, and then they want it more."

"When you sign a pledge to your father to preserve your virginity, your sexuality is basically being taken away from you until you sign yet another contract, a marital one," worries Eve Ensler, the writer and activist. "It makes you feel like you're the least important person in the whole equation. It makes you feel invisible."

It's not hard to imagine the anxiety young women must feel about being a purity failure. Carol-Maureen, an acquaintance from my hometown of Fargo, North Dakota, who got a purity ring in seventh grade and still wears it at 22, told me, "If I had sex before marriage and my parents found out, I'd be mortified. I'd feel like I failed in this promise to them, even though it's really not their business."

Marie, a Texan I met through a colleague, took a virginity pledge at 14 but actually felt no shame about breaking her vow a year later. "When I took the pledge, I was true in my heart, but as I got older I had a broader world view," she says. Still, she snuck around to have sex with her boyfriend so her parents wouldn't find out, and ended up getting pregnant at 19; she married quickly thereafter. Would she ever ask her son to take a virginity pledge? "No," she says. "I don't want him to tell me something just because he thinks I want to hear it and then lie to me about it."

Figuring out your sexuality on your own terms is a major passage into adulthood. Back when I was 19 and contemplating having sex for the first time, I presented my virginity to my boyfriend as this great treasure he could take from me. He looked at me and said, "But I don't want to take anything. You should be having sex with me because you want to—and if you don't, then you aren't ready." I was embarrassed by the smack-down of my "gift," but his words made me realize sex wasn't just something to give to him but something to do for myself, too. Learning that was more meaningful to me than actually having sex.

When I point out to Christy Parcha's father, Mike, that experience with relationships, bumps and all, can help young women mature emotionally and become ready for sex and marriage, he warily concedes that's true. "But there can be damage, too," he says. "I guess we'd rather err on the side of avoiding these things. The girl can learn after marriage." Like other fathers I speak with, Parcha says that if his daughter were to fail in her quest to be pure, she would be met with "grace and forgiveness."

But, he continues, "I am not worried about that. She is not even going to come close to those situations. She believes, and I do too, that her husband will come through our family connections or through me before her heart even gets involved." Randy Wilson's oldest daughter, Lauren, 22, met her fiancé, Brett, a young man from the Air Force Academy, at church, and other fathers and daughters mention this to me as a hopeful sign that God will open similar doors for them. God has been throwing some curveballs lately, though; a week before the ball, Mike and Christy Parcha's pastor, Ted Haggard, a man who has openly railed against gay marriage, made headlines nationwide when he admitted to receiving a massage from a man (one who claimed Haggard had paid him for sex), showing how at odds what is preached and what is practiced can be.

Following dessert—chocolate cake or fruit coulis for the adults, ice cream sundaes for the girls—couples file into the adjacent ballroom. Seven ballerinas, including Christy Parcha, appear in white gowns with tulle skirts, carrying on their shoulders a large, rustic wooden cross that they lift up and rest on a stand. Lisa Wilson cries as she presents each of their three ceremonial dances, one of which is called "I'll Always Be Your Baby." Afterward, Randy Wilson and a fellow pastor, Steve Holt, stand at the cross with heavy rapiers raised and announce that they are prepared to "bear swords and war for the hearts of our daughters." The blades create an inverted "V" under which girls and fathers kneel and lay white roses that symbolize purity. Soon there is a heap of cream-colored buds wilting beneath the outstretched arms of the cross.

It's a memorable image at the end of a memorable night. I've been moved and charmed by the Wilsons, an uncommonly warm, polite and loving brood. Over and over, the five daughters have told me how great their father is at giving them attention, love and hugs. When Khrystian ballroom-dances with him, they look so comfortable in each other's arms that you wish every girl in the United States could have that closeness.

But the real challenge, in my mind, is for a father to remain loving toward his daughter and at the same time nurture her autonomy. The purity movement is, in essence, about refusing to let girls grow up: Daddy's girls never have to be adults. "The balls are saying, I want you to be 11 forever," says Kindlon. These are girls who may never find out what it means to make decisions without a man involved, to stand up for themselves, to own their sexuality.

I deeply wish that the lovely things I have seen tonight—the delighted young women, the caring, doting dads—might evolve into father-daughter events not tied to exhorting a promise from a girl that may hang over her head as she struggles to become a woman. When Lauren Wilson hit adolescence, her father gave her a purity ring and a charm necklace with a tiny lock and key. Randy Wilson took the key, which he will hand over to her husband on their wedding day. The image of a locked area behind which a girl stores all of her messy desires until one day a man comes along with the key haunts me. By the end of the ball, as I watch fathers carrying out sleepy little girls with drooping tiaras and enveloping older girls with wraps, I want to take every one of those girls aside and whisper to them the real secret of womanhood: The key to any treasure you've got is held by one person—you.

Questions for 6.1

1. What is the purpose of having young girls participate in purity balls and make purity vows?
2. What do you think motivates young girls to take such vows?
3. What do you think motivates fathers to encourage their daughters to participate?
4. How important is the exchange of rings to the event? What are its implications?
5. Is making a purity vow a way to empower girls and women or does it disempower them?
6. How much money has been allocated nationally to fund abstinence-only sex education programs? How does this sum compare to sex education funding? Can you find the figures and compare them?
7. Why are STD rates significantly higher in communities that have a high proportion of pledgers?
8. Why do people who advocate abstinence discourage providing young people with information about sex and contraception? Is this a good way to protect girls and women?
9. What does the author mean when she says that figuring out sexuality on your own terms is a major passage into adulthood? Do you agree or disagree? Explain your answer.
10. Explain the military symbolism and other symbols that are used in the purity balls.
11. What do you think is the best way to limit unintended pregnancies and decrease STD rates?
12. Why do the fathers who participate in the purity balls think they are a good idea?
13. What might be the detrimental effect of encouraging such a ritual?

Red Sex, Blue Sex

Margaret Talbot

Why do so many evangelical teen-agers become pregnant?

In early September, when Sarah Palin, the Republican candidate for Vice-President, announced that her unwed seventeen-year-old daughter, Bristol, was pregnant, many liberals were shocked, not by the revelation but by the reaction to it. They expected the news to dismay the evangelical voters that John McCain was courting with his choice of Palin. Yet reports from the floor of the Republican Convention, in St. Paul, quoted dozens of delegates who seemed unfazed, or even buoyed, by the news. A delegate from Louisiana told CBS News, "Like so many other American families who are in the same situation, I think it's great that she instilled in her daughter the values to have the child and not to sneak off someplace and have an abortion." A Mississippi delegate claimed that "even though young children are making that decision to become pregnant, they've also decided to take responsibility for their actions and decided to follow up with that and get married and raise this child." Palin's family drama, delegates said, was similar to the experience of many socially conservative Christian families. As Marlys Popma, the head of evangelical outreach for the McCain campaign, told *National Review,* "There hasn't been one evangelical family that hasn't gone through some sort of situation." In fact, it was Popma's own "crisis pregnancy" that had brought her into the movement in the first place.

Selection 6.2

During the campaign, the media has largely respected calls to treat Bristol Palin's pregnancy as a private matter. But the reactions to it have exposed a cultural rift that mirrors America's dominant political divide. Social liberals in the country's "blue states" tend to support sex education and are not particularly troubled by the idea that many teen-agers have sex before marriage, but would regard a teen-age daughter's pregnancy as devastating news. And the social conservatives in "red states" generally advocate abstinence-only education and denounce sex before marriage, but are relatively unruffled if a teen-ager becomes pregnant, as long as she doesn't choose to have an abortion.

A handful of social scientists and family-law scholars have recently begun looking closely at this split. Last year, Mark Regnerus, a sociologist at the University of Texas at Austin, published a startling book called "Forbidden Fruit:

Sex and Religion in the Lives of American Teenagers," and he is working on a follow-up that includes a section titled "Red Sex, Blue Sex." His findings are drawn from a national survey that Regnerus and his colleagues conducted of some thirty-four hundred thirteen-to-seventeen-year-olds, and from a comprehensive government study of adolescent health known as Add Health. Regnerus argues that religion is a good indicator of attitudes toward sex, but a poor one of sexual behavior, and that this gap is especially wide among teen-agers who identify themselves as evangelical. The vast majority of white evangelical adolescents—seventy-four per cent—say that they believe in abstaining from sex before marriage. (Only half of mainline Protestants, and a quarter of Jews, say that they believe in abstinence.) Moreover, among the major religious groups, evangelical virgins are the least likely to anticipate that sex will be pleasurable, and the most likely to believe that having sex will cause their partners to lose respect for them. (Jews most often cite pleasure as a reason to have sex, and say that an unplanned pregnancy would be an embarrassment.) But, according to Add Health data, evangelical teen-agers are more sexually active than Mormons, mainline Protestants, and Jews. On average, white evangelical Protestants make their "sexual début"—to use the festive term of social-science researchers—shortly after turning sixteen. Among major religious groups, only black Protestants begin having sex earlier.

Another key difference in behavior, Regnerus reports, is that evangelical Protestant teen-agers are significantly less likely than other groups to use contraception. This could be because evangelicals are also among the most likely to believe that using contraception will send the message that they are looking for sex. It could also be because many evangelicals are steeped in the abstinence movement's warnings that condoms won't actually protect them from pregnancy or venereal disease. More provocatively, Regnerus found that only half of sexually active teen-agers who say that they seek guidance from God or the Scriptures when making a tough decision report using contraception every time. By contrast, sixty-nine per cent of sexually active youth who say that they most often follow the counsel of a parent or another trusted adult consistently use protection.

The gulf between sexual belief and sexual behavior becomes apparent, too, when you look at the outcomes of abstinence-pledge movements. Nationwide, according to a 2001 estimate, some two and a half million people have taken a pledge to remain celibate until marriage. Usually, they do so under the auspices of movements such as True Love Waits or the Silver Ring Thing. Sometimes, they make their vows at big rallies featuring Christian pop stars and laser light shows, or at purity balls, where girls in frothy dresses exchange rings with their fathers, who vow to help them remain virgins until the day they marry. More than half of those who take such pledges—which, unlike abstinence-only classes in public schools, are explicitly Christian—end up having sex before marriage, and not usually with their future spouse. The movement is not the complete washout its critics portray it as: pledgers delay sex eighteen months longer than non-pledgers, and have fewer partners. Yet, according to the sociologists Peter Bearman, of Columbia University, and Hannah Brückner, of Yale, communities with high rates of pledging also have high rates of S.T.D.s. This could be because more teens pledge in communities where they perceive more danger from sex (in which case the pledge is doing some good); or it could be because fewer people in these communities use condoms when they break the pledge.

Bearman and Brückner have also identified a peculiar dilemma: in some schools, if too many teens pledge, the effort basically collapses. Pledgers apparently gather strength from the sense that they are an embattled minority; once their numbers exceed thirty per cent, and proclaimed chastity becomes the norm, that special identity is lost. With such a fragile formula, it's hard to imagine how educators can ever get it right: once the self-proclaimed virgin clique hits the thirty-one-per-cent mark, suddenly it's Sodom and Gomorrah.

Religious belief apparently does make a potent difference in behavior for one group of evangelical teen-agers: those who score highest on measures of religiosity—such as how often they go to church, or how often they pray at home. But many Americans who identify themselves as evangelicals, and who hold socially conservative beliefs, aren't deeply observant.

Even more important than religious conviction, Regnerus argues, is how "embedded" a teen-ager is in a network of friends, family, and institutions that reinforce his or her goal of delaying sex, and that offer a plausible alternative to America's sexed-up consumer culture. A church, of course, isn't the only way to provide a cohesive sense of community. Close-knit families make a difference. Teen-agers who live with both biological parents are more likely to be virgins than those who do not. And adolescents who say that their families understand them, pay attention to their concerns, and have fun with them are more likely to delay intercourse, regardless of religiosity.

A terrific 2005 documentary, "The Education of Shelby Knox," tells the story of a teen-ager from a Southern Baptist family in Lubbock, Texas, who has taken a True Love Waits pledge. To the chagrin of her youth pastor, and many of her neighbors, Knox eventually becomes an activist for comprehensive sex education. At her high school, kids receive abstinence-only education, but, Knox says, "maybe twice a week I see a girl walking down the hall pregnant." In the film, Knox seems successful at remaining chaste, but less because she took a pledge than because she has a fearlessly independent mind and the kind of parents who—despite their own conservative leanings—admire her outspokenness. Devout Republicans, her parents end up driving her around town to make speeches that would have curled their hair before their daughter started making them. Her mother even comes to take pride in Shelby's efforts, because while abstinence pledges are lovely in the abstract, they don't acknowledge "reality."

Like other American teens, young evangelicals live in a world of Internet porn, celebrity sex scandals, and raunchy reality TV, and they have the same hormonal urges that their peers have. Yet they come from families and communities in which sexual life is supposed to be forestalled until the first night of a transcendent honeymoon. Regnerus writes, "In such an atmosphere, attitudes about sex may *formally* remain unchanged (and restrictive) while sexual activity becomes increasingly common. This clash of cultures and norms is felt most poignantly in the so-called Bible Belt." Symbolic commitment to the institution of marriage remains strong there, and politically motivating—hence the drive to outlaw gay marriage—but the actual practice of it is scattershot.

Among blue-state social liberals, commitment to the institution of marriage tends to be unspoken or discreet, but marriage in practice typically works pretty well. Two family-law scholars, Naomi Cahn, of George Washington University, and June Carbone, of the University of Missouri at Kansas City, are writing a book on the subject, and they argue that "red families" and "blue families" are "living different lives, with different moral imperatives." (They emphasize that the Republican-Democrat divide is less important than the higher concentration of "moral-values voters" in red states.) In 2004, the states with the highest divorce rates were Nevada, Arkansas, Wyoming, Idaho, and West Virginia (all red states in the 2004 election); those with the lowest were Illinois, Massachusetts, Iowa, Minnesota, and New Jersey. The highest teen-pregnancy rates were in Nevada, Arizona, Mississippi, New Mexico, and Texas (all red); the lowest were in North Dakota, Vermont, New Hampshire, Minnesota, and Maine (blue except for North Dakota). "The 'blue states' of the Northeast and Mid-Atlantic have lower teen birthrates, higher use of abortion, and lower percentages of teen births within marriage," Cahn and Carbone observe. They also note that people start families earlier in red states—in part because they are more inclined to deal with an unplanned pregnancy by marrying rather than by seeking an abortion.

Of all variables, the age at marriage may be the pivotal difference between red and blue families. The five states with the lowest median age at marriage are Utah, Oklahoma, Idaho, Arkansas, and Kentucky, all red states, while those with the highest are all blue: Massachusetts, New York, Rhode Island, Connecticut, and New Jersey. The red-state model puts couples at greater risk for divorce; women who marry before their mid-twenties are significantly more likely to divorce than those who marry later. And younger couples are more likely to be contending with two of the biggest stressors on a marriage: financial struggles and the birth of a baby before, or soon after, the wedding.

There are, of course, plenty of exceptions to these rules—messily divorcing professional couples in Boston, high-school sweethearts who stay sweetly together in rural Idaho. Still, Cahn and Carbone conclude, "the paradigmatic red-state couple enters marriage not long after the woman becomes sexually active, has two children by her mid-twenties, and reaches the critical period of marriage at the high point in the life cycle for risk-taking and experimentation. The paradigmatic blue-state couple is more likely to experiment with multiple partners, postpone marriage until after they reach emotional and financial maturity, and have their children (if they have them at all) as their lives are stabilizing."

Some of these differences in sexual behavior come down to class and education. Regnerus and Carbone and Cahn all see a new and distinct "middle-class morality" taking shape among economically and socially advantaged families who are not social conservatives. In Regnerus's survey, the teen-agers who espouse this new morality are tolerant of premarital sex (and of contraception and abortion) but are themselves cautious about pursuing it. Regnerus writes, "They are interested in remaining free from the burden of teenage pregnancy and the sorrows and embarrassments of sexually transmitted diseases. They perceive a bright future for themselves, one with college, advanced degrees, a career, and a family. Simply put, too much seems at stake. Sexual intercourse is not worth the risks." These are the kids who tend to score high on measures of "strategic orientation"—how analytical, methodical, and fact-seeking they are when making decisions. Because these teen-agers see abstinence as unrealistic, they are not opposed in principle to sex before marriage—just careful about it. Accordingly, they might delay intercourse in favor of oral sex, not because they cherish the idea of remaining "technical virgins" but because they assess it as a safer option. "Solidly middle- or upper-middle-class adolescents have considerable socioeconomic and educational expectations, courtesy of their parents and their communities' lifestyles," Regnerus writes. "They are happy with their direction, generally not rebellious, tend to get along with their parents, and have few moral qualms about expressing their nascent sexuality." They might have loved Ellen

Page in "Juno," but in real life they'd see having a baby at the wrong time as a tragic derailment of their life plans. For this group, Regnerus says, unprotected sex has become "a moral issue like smoking or driving a car without a seatbelt. It's not just unwise anymore; it's wrong."

Each of these models of sexual behavior has drawbacks—in the blue-state scheme, people may postpone child-bearing to the point where infertility becomes an issue. And delaying child-bearing is better suited to the more affluent, for whom it yields economic benefits, in the form of educational opportunities and career advancement. But Carbone and Cahn argue that the red-state model is clearly failing on its own terms—producing high rates of teen pregnancy, divorce, sexually transmitted disease, and other dysfunctional outcomes that social conservatives say they abhor. In "Forbidden Fruit," Regnerus offers an "unscientific postscript," in which he advises social conservatives that if they really want to maintain their commitment to chastity and to marriage, they'll need to do more to help young couples stay married longer. As the Reverend Rick Marks, a Southern Baptist minister, recently pointed out in a Florida newspaper, "Evangelicals are fighting gay marriage, saying it will break down traditional marriage, when divorce has already broken it down." Conservatives may need to start talking as much about saving marriages as they do about, say, saving oneself for marriage.

"Having to wait until age twenty-five or thirty to have sex *is* unreasonable," Regnerus writes. He argues that religious organizations that advocate chastity should "work more creatively to support younger marriages. This is not the 1950s (for which I am glad), where one could bank on social norms, extended (and larger) families, and clear gender roles to negotiate and sustain early family formation."

Evangelicals could start, perhaps, by trying to untangle the contradictory portrayals of sex that they offer to teen-agers. In the Shelby Knox documentary, a youth pastor, addressing an assembly of teens, defines intercourse as "what two dogs do out on the street corner—they just bump and grind awhile, *boom boom boom*." Yet a typical evangelical text aimed at young people, "Every Young Woman's Battle," by Shannon Ethridge and Stephen Arterburn, portrays sex between two virgins as an ethereal communion of innocent souls: "physical, mental, emotional, and spiritual pleasure beyond description." Neither is the most realistic or helpful view for a young person to take into marriage, as a few advocates of abstinence acknowledge. The savvy young Christian writer Lauren Winner, in her book "Real Sex: The Naked Truth About Chastity," writes, "Rather than spending our unmarried years stewarding and disciplining our desires, we have become ashamed of them. We persuade ourselves that the desires themselves are horrible. This can have real consequences if we do get married." Teenagers and single adults are "told over and over not to have sex, but no one ever encourages" them "to be bodily or sensual in some appropriate way"—getting to know and appreciate what their bodies can do through sports, especially for girls, or even thinking sensually about something like food. Winner goes on, "This doesn't mean, of course, that if only the church sponsored more softball leagues, everyone would stay on the chaste straight and narrow. But it does mean that the church ought to cultivate ways of teaching Christians to live in their bodies well— so that unmarried folks can still be bodily people, even though they're not having sex, and so that married people can give themselves to sex freely."

Too often, though, evangelical literature directed at teen-agers forbids all forms of sexual behavior, even masturbation. "Every Young Woman's Battle," for example, tells teen-agers that "the momentary relief" of "self-gratification" can lead to "shame, low self-esteem, and fear of what others might think or that something is wrong with you." And it won't slake sexual desire: "Once you begin feeding baby monsters, their appetites grow bigger and they want MORE! It's better not to feed such a monster in the first place."

Shelby Knox, who spoke at a congressional hearing on sex education earlier this year, occupies a middle ground. She testified that it's possible to "believe in abstinence in a religious sense," but still understand that abstinence-only education is dangerous "for students who simply are not abstaining." As Knox's approach makes clear, you don't need to break out the sex toys to teach sex ed—you can encourage teen-agers to postpone sex for all kinds of practical, emotional, and moral reasons. A new "abstinence-plus" curriculum, now growing in popularity, urges abstinence while providing accurate information about contraception and reproduction for those who have sex anyway. "Abstinence works," Knox said at the hearing. "Abstinence-only-until-marriage does not."

It might help, too, not to present virginity as the cornerstone of a virtuous life. In certain evangelical circles, the concept is so emphasized that a girl who regrets having been sexually active is encouraged to declare herself a "secondary" or "born-again" virgin. That's not an idea, surely, that helps teen-agers postpone sex or have it responsibly.

The "pro-family" efforts of social conservatives—the campaigns against gay marriage and abortion—do nothing to instill the emotional discipline or the psychological smarts that forsaking all others often involves. Evangelicals are very good at articulating their sexual ideals, but they have little practical advice for their young followers. Social liberals, meanwhile, are not very good at articulating values on marriage and teen sexuality—indeed, they may feel that it's unseemly or judgmental to do so. But in fact the new middle-class morality is squarely pro-family. Maybe these choices weren't originally about values—maybe they were about maximizing education and careers—yet the result is a more stable family system. Not only do couples who marry later stay married longer; children born to older couples fare better on a variety of measures, including educational attainment, regardless of their parents' economic circumstances. The new middle-class culture of intensive parenting has ridiculous aspects, but it's pretty successful at turning out productive, emotionally resilient young adults. And its intensity may be one reason that teenagers from close families see child-rearing as a project for which they're not yet ready. For too long, the conventional wisdom has been that social conservatives are the upholders of family values, whereas liberals are the proponents of a polymorphous selfishness. This isn't true, and, every once in a while, liberals might point that out.

Some evangelical Christians are starting to reckon with the failings of the preaching-and-pledging approach. In "The Education of Shelby Knox," for example, Shelby's father is uncomfortable, at first, with his daughter's campaign. Lubbock, after all, is a town so conservative that its local youth pastor tells Shelby, "You ask me sometimes why I look at you a little funny. It's because I hear you speak and I hear tolerance." But as her father listens to her arguments he realizes that the no-tolerance ethic simply hasn't worked in their deeply Christian community. Too many girls in town are having sex, and having babies that they can't support. As Shelby's father declares toward the end of the film, teen-age pregnancy "is a problem—a major, major problem that everybody's just shoving under the rug."

Questions for 6.2

1. Explain the nature of the "cultural rift" described in this article.
2. What does Mark Regnerus, quoted in this article, mean when he says that "religion is a good indicator of attitudes toward sex, but a poor one of sexual behavior"?
3. What evidence does he provide for this claim?
4. According to this author, white evangelical Protestant girls become sexually active earlier than most other girls. Why is this significant?
5. What is the attitude toward the use of contraceptives described in this article? Does this population tend to use contraceptives?
6. What factors come into play in determining when teens become sexually active?

7. What variables seem to have to the most significance in explaining cultural differences among teens?

8. According to this article, how do differences in class and education explain differences in sexual behavior?

9. Why does Shelby Knox say that "abstinence" works while "abstinence-only-until-marriage" doesn't?

10. What is the relationship between marrying later and having a more stable family system?

11. Does the author agree or disagree with the claim that conservatives are the ones who uphold family values? How does he explain his position?

12. Why do so many evangelical teenagers become pregnant?

Is the Pope Crazy?

Katha Pollitt

There are many things to be said against condoms, and most people reading this have probably said them all. But at least they work. Not perfectly—they slip, they break, they require more forethought and finesse and cooperation and trust than is easy to bring to sex every single time, and, a major drawback in this fallen world, they place women's safety in the hands of men. But for birth control they are a whole lot better than the rhythm method or prayer or nothing, and for protection from sexually transmitted diseases they are all we have. This is not exactly a controversial statement; people have been using condoms as a barrier against disease as long as rubber has been around (indeed, before—as readers of James Boswell's journals know). You could ask a thousand doctors—ten thousand doctors—before you'd find one who said, Condoms? Don't bother.

Selection 6.3

But what do doctors know? Or the Centers for Disease Control, or the World Health Organization, or the American Foundation for AIDS Research (Amfar)? These days, the experts on condoms are politicians, preachers and priests, and the word from above is: Condoms don't work. That is what students are being taught in the abstinence-only sex ed favored by the religious right and funded by the Bush Administration—$117 million of your annual tax dollars at work. The theory is that even mentioning condoms, much less admitting that they dramatically reduce the chances of pregnancy or HIV infection, sends a "mixed message" about the value of total abstinence until marriage. How absurd—it's like saying that seat belts send a mixed message about the speed limit or vitamin pills send a mixed message about vegetables. Anti-condom propaganda can backfire, too: True, some kids may be scared away from sex, although probably not until marriage; others, though, hear only a reason to throw caution to the winds. According to a 2002 Human Rights Watch report on abstinence-only sex ed in Texas, a condoms-don't-work ad campaign led sexually active teens to have unprotected sex: "My boyfriend says they don't work. He heard it on the radio." Why is the Bush Administration giving horny teenage boys an excuse to be sexually selfish? You might as well have high school teachers telling them using a condom during sex is like taking a shower in a raincoat.

Now it seems the Vatican is joining fundamentalist Protestants to spread the word against condoms around the globe. "To talk of condoms as 'safe sex' is a form of Russian roulette," said Alfonso Lopez Trujillo, head of the Vatican's office on the family. On the BBC *Panorama* program "Sex and the Holy City," Lopez Trujillo explained, "The AIDS virus is roughly 450 times smaller than the spermatozoon. The spermatozoon can easily pass through the 'net' that is formed by the condom." That latex has holes or pores through which HIV (or sperm) can pass is a total canard. A National Institutes of Health panel that included anti-condom advocates examined the effectiveness of condoms from just about every perspective, including strength and porosity; according to its report, released in July 2001, latex condoms are impermeable to even the smallest pathogen. Among STDs, HIV is actually the one condoms work best against. "We're all a bit stunned by Lopez Trujillo's lack of respect for scientific consensus," Dr. Judith Auerbach of Amfar, who sat on the NIH panel, told me. "Where do his numbers come from?" Is Lopez Trujillo, who even suggests putting warnings on condoms like those on cigarettes, a loose cannon such as can be found in even the best regulated bureaucracies? According to "Sex and the Holy City," in Africa, where HIV infects millions—20 percent in Kenya, 40 percent in Botswana, 34 percent in Zimbabwe—Catholic clergy, who oppose condoms as they do all contraception, are actively promoting the myth that condoms don't prevent transmission of the virus and may even spread it. The *Guardian* quotes the archbishop of Nairobi, Raphael Ndingi Nzeki, as saying: "AIDS . . . has grown so fast because of the availability of condoms." Thus is a decade of painstaking work to mainstream and normalize condom use undone by the conscious promotion of an urban legend.

When the Nobel Prize for Peace was awarded to Shirin Ebadi, the first ever to a Muslim woman, an Iranian and a crusader for women's rights, not everyone was thrilled. What about Pope John Paul II, now celebrating the twenty-fifth anniversary of his election, and possibly near death? "This . . . was his year," wrote David Brooks in his *New York Times* column, a hymn of praise for the Pope as the defender of "the whole and the indivisible dignity of each person." A few pages over, Peter Steinfels said much the same in his religion column: "Is there any other leader who has so reshaped the political world for the better and done it peacefully?" More knowledgeable people than I can debate how much credit the Pope should get for the fall of Communism—I always thought it was Ronald Reagan with an unintentional assist from Gorbachev plus the internal collapse of the system itself. With the crucial exception of Poland, the countries in the old Soviet bloc aren't even Roman Catholic, or are so only partially. Whatever his contribution to that historic set of events, though, the Pope is on the wrong side of history now.

Women's equality, sexual rights for all, the struggle of the individual against authoritarian religion and of course the global AIDS epidemic—the Pope has been a disaster on all these crucial issues of our new century. It's all very well for David Brooks to mock those who [criticize] the Pope for his "unfashionable views on abortion," as if 78,000 women a year dying in illegal procedures around the world was just something to chat about over brie and chablis. But add it up: a priesthood as male as the Kuwaiti electorate—even altar girls may be banned soon, according to one recent news story—no divorce, no abortion, no contraception, no condom use even within a faithful marriage to prevent a deadly infection.

It's bad enough to argue that condoms are against God's will while millions die. But to maintain, falsely, that they are ineffective in order to discourage their use is truly immoral. If not insane.

Questions for 6.3

1. Why do people use condoms?
2. Is condom use an effective way of preventing pregnancies and STDs?
3. Is condom use an effective way of preventing the spread of HIV and AIDS?
4. Who opposes condom use? Be specific.
5. What does Pollitt mean when she refers to an "urban legend"?
6. Why does Pollitt say that discouraging the use of condoms is immoral if not insane? Do you agree or disagree? Explain your answer.

"Hello Central, Give Me Heaven"

When I was considerably younger and very interested in performing, I was in a school play that included the song "Hello Central, Give Me Heaven," written and published in 1901 by Charlie Harris and later made popular by the Carter Family. Thinking of the song now, so many years later, still makes me smile. The refrain goes like this:

> *Hello central give me heaven*
> *For I know my mother's there*
> *And you'll find her with the angels*
> *Over on the golden stair*

Yes, I confess it, there is something comforting about the possibility of communicating directly with loved ones now departed. And placing the song in its historical context should remind us of the time in the early part of the twentieth century when the growing spread of telephones raised all sorts of questions, possibilities, and perhaps hopes. But the important questions that arise from this memory should ask what problems are solved by assuaging your anxiety or sadness in this way, even assuming that that were possible.

The first article in this chapter is appropriately titled "Moms in Touch with God." I say appropriately because it seems to be an extension of the perspective or hope expressed in "Hello Central." In both cases, the people involved seem to take what begins as a charming hope or desire and turn it into something to be taken literally. The women described in this article (which is subjected to no critical analysis of any kind) wanted to protect their children and decided that praying in an organized way was the way to do it. According to the reporter, about 1000 New Jersey mothers participate in Moms in Touch with God.

The second article examines the link between the mind and the body and the mind's alleged ability to affect the body's behavior. Peggy Orenstein, the author of this article, stops in her tracks when she sees a sign in a store window that announces, "Stress is related to 99 percent of all illness." In trying to understand why people would be interested in placing "the locus of illness in their heads rather than their bodies" she comes up with several possibilities, including the possibility that the ailments that women in particular are prone to—reproductive cancers, arthritis, fibromyalgia—may be the result of our rapid social progress.

Orenstein refers to this point of view as "double magical thinking." She reports that a Canadian study done in 2001 found that almost two-thirds of the 200 survivors of ovarian cancer attributed their survival to a positive attitude—unlike Orenstein herself, who was more inclined to attribute it to just plain good luck.

The final article in this chapter, "Is Prayer Good for Your Health?" directly confronts the question the title asks. The article reports on a number of studies that took the question seriously, studies that constructed elaborate double-blind experiments that explored such questions as whether "distant intercessory prayer" has an effect. Read the accounts of these studies and then use critical thinking to evaluate their conclusions.

Further Reading

Angelos, James. "Answered Prayers." *New York Times,* September 14, 2008.

Caret, Benedict. "Can Prayers Heal? Critics Say Studies Go Past Science's Reach." *New York Times,* October 10, 2004.

Caret, Benedict. "Long-Awaited Medical Study Questions the Power of Prayer," *New York Times,* March 31, 2006.

"Plan Endless Prayers: Victory Supplication to be Continuous 24 Hours Every Day." *New York Times,* June 9, 1918.

Moms in Touch with God

Tanya Drobness

At the time, Margo Walter didn't know why.

The night before she left home for Vanderbilt University in 1976, Walter's mother took her across the den where she had been packing and sat her down on the couch. She put her hands on her shoulders and began to pray.

The next day, on campus, Walter met the man who would become her husband, Frank.

"I didn't know what she was doing, but now I understand it," Walter said of her praying mother.

As a mother of a Montclair [New Jersey] Kimberley Academy student and two college-age sons, Walter, 50, was prompted to find a way to pray more intensely for her own children, particularly after she put her son Joe on a school bus

Selection 7.1

to Nishuane Elementary School. He came home crying because one kid paid another kid $1 to sock him in the stomach.

"I realized then that there was no way I could protect him on the bus, and I realized I needed to pray," said Walter, who is now the New Jersey state coordinator for Moms In Touch International, a worldwide Christian-based organization that gathers mothers together in their towns so they can pray for their children and schools.

The organization's Web site, www.momsintouch.org, will provide a link to a newly created Web page of the New Jersey branch beginning tomorrow, Friday, Aug. 1. It will include events, accept submissions for prayer requests, [reprint] Walter's monthly newsletter and provide contact information, she said.

"What women can do is unload some of the burden unto God, and find comfort so they can continue to parent their children with confidence and with joy," Walter told The [Montclair] Times.

The New Jersey branch of the organization, which has been growing in participation, was mostly formed in Montclair in 2002, stemming from the international organization that has been in existence since 1984.

The organization's founder, Fern Nichols, started the group after sending her sons off to junior high school, apprehensive of outside influences and the people who would guide her children.

Today, mothers in more than 120 countries gather, usually once a week, in private homes to pray in a Moms In Touch group. There are Moms In

"Moms in Touch with God: Praying for the Protection of Children and Schools," by Tanya Drobness, *Montclair* [N.J.] *Times,* July 3, 2008.
Reprinted with permission by Tanya Drobness.

Touch booklets available in 38 languages that help bring Christian moms to-gether, even in countries where missionaries are not allowed.

In Montclair, 42 women participate in Moms In Touch groups that are set up to pray for specific schools, but the schools have no affiliation with them and the mothers do not advocate prayer in school, Walter said.

"We simply serve the schools by praying," she said. "We put prayer back in by praying, not by changing the law."

Though mothers "pray in the name of Jesus," the group is open to any mother, regardless of religious affiliation, who wants to pray for [her] chil-dren with other mothers.

About 1,000 New Jersey mothers participate in Moms In Touch. The mothers pray on behalf of 384 of the state's approximately 3,800 public and private schools, colleges and universities, Walter said.

"You can pray by yourself, but it's easier when women come by your side and partner with you to do it," Walter said. "It builds deep bonds of friend-ship," she added, noting that confidentiality is a main building block of the group. Prayer topics can range from praying for teachers and sports events to resolving drug-related problems.

For about one hour, prayers are conducted in four phases: Praise to God as good; silent confessions; thanksgiving to remember what God has given; and intercession to pray for someone else.

Walter said she recites a familiar prayer regularly for her children, so they are always reminded of God's goodness, from a Bible verse, Philippians 2:13: "For it is God who works in you to will and to act according to His good purpose."

For more information about Moms In Touch International, visit the Web site or call Walter at 973-783-5765.

Questions for 7.1

1. Why was the organization Moms in Touch with God formed?
2. What does Margo Walter believe is the relationship between her mother's pray-ing to God the night before she left for college and the man she met on cam-pus the next day? What evidence does she present for her belief?
3. Why does Walter believe that she can protect her sons by praying?
4. What evidence does she present for her belief?
5. What, according to Walker, is the general benefit of praying to God?
6. What kinds of prayer topics do Moms in Touch with God adopt?
7. Do these topics seem appropriate things for prayer?
8. What does Walter believe is the benefit of women coming together to pray?
9. What are other ways that parents can protect their children? Evaluate their effectiveness.

Stress Test

Why Americans Want to Believe That Our Mental States Can Control Our Physical Maladies

Peggy Orenstein

For weeks before a store down the street from where I live in Berkeley opened, it was unclear what it would sell—materially, anyway. Rather than having a sign describing the merchandise, the windows were papered over with foot-high aphorisms in punchy red and white type. "Friends are more important than money." "Jealousy works the opposite way you want it to." True enough, I suppose. But the one that caught my attention was this: "Stress is related to 99 percent of all illness."

I tried to imagine how that claim made it past the copywriters and project managers who must have approved

Selection 7.2

it. It was hardly as benign as the suggestions that people should floss daily or drink lots of water. Or was it? Somewhere along the line, maybe when yoga studios began to outnumber Starbucks outlets, the notion, at once modern and primitive, of the mind's irrefutable power over the flesh became the conventional wisdom.

It's not that I think the mind-body connection is a total sham. But even where it would seem most established, say in the relationship between stress and heart disease, the mechanism is unclear. Is stress an independent risk factor or does it merely influence others, raising blood pressure or encouraging over-eating? Either way, popular mythology both simplifies and generalizes the potential harm, applying it to everything that ails us. After all, it *feels* true: I'm more at peace with my frenetic life after a few rounds of sun salutations. Yet, what does that prove?

Admittedly, I'm a tad touchy about this. Eleven years (and, as of this writing, 6 months, 2 days, 19 hours and 30 minutes) ago I found out I had breast cancer. I later endured years of multiple miscarriages and failed infertility treatments before conceiving a child. So I've fielded my share of intimations that stress, or some other self-inflicted wrong thinking, could be the source of my troubles: I should relax, take a vacation, express my anger. I do my best. In a nod to that latter advice, I yelled at the screen during *Sex and the City* when Charlotte, who has an adopted Chinese daughter, becomes unexpectedly pregnant and explains: "People always say that when you stop trying it can happen. My doctor says that she knows other couples who've adopted, and then they get pregnant."

The idea that easing up on the pressure kick-starts women's fertility intuitively seems sound. Everyone knows someone (or someone who knows someone) who gave birth after adopting. From the 1930s through 1950s, according to *The Empty Cradle,* a history of infertility, medical literature actually promoted adoption as a "cure," claiming it resulted in pregnancy "more often than not." Freudians, too, counseled that infertility was psychological, the result of maternal ambivalence; resolve those feelings through adoption, and fecundity would follow.

Except—leaving aside the insinuations that adoption is a means to an end rather than its own joyous experience, and that women who become easily pregnant are never ambivalent—it's not true. As early as 1949, a study of adoptive parents co-written by the infertility pioneer John Rock showed they conceived at the same rate as nonadopting infertile couples: around 10 percent. (Subsequent research has put the likelihood as low as 3 percent.) What's more, according to a 2005 study of women undergoing in vitro fertilization, published in the journal *Human Reproduction,* stress had no impact on pregnancy rates. The fretful conceived as readily as the chill.

I suspect women today may be particularly vulnerable to placing the locus of illness in their heads rather than their bodies. In part that's because the causes of the ailments we're prone to—reproductive cancers, arthritis, fibromyalgia—are often mysterious in origin. But it may also be an artifact of our rapid and successful social progress. We of the postfeminist generation grew up being told we could do anything, be anything, if we just put our minds to it. Yet, if we have the power to create our own fates, wouldn't the corollary be that we're also responsible for our own misfortunes? And, in a kind of double magical thinking, shouldn't we be able to cure ourselves using the same indefatigable will? No surprise, then, that in a 2001 Canadian study of 200 ovarian-cancer survivors, almost two-thirds believed that stress caused their disease and more than 80 percent attributed their survival to a positive attitude. A related study of women who had breast cancer produced similar results—fewer than 5 percent chalked up their survival to any medical treatment. Or (as I do) to just plain good luck. Meanwhile, a Danish study of 6,689 women, published in 2005, found those who were highly stressed were 40 percent less likely than others to get breast cancer.

Susan Sontag noted that a culture's maladies are apparent in the emotional causes it attributes to illness. In the Victorian period, cancer was "caused" by excessive family obligations or hyper-emotionalism. In the 1970s it was "caused" by isolation and suppressed anger. So the assertion that stress underlies 99 percent of illness may indicate more about the healthy than the sick. Stress is our burden, our bogyman, and reducing it is the latest all-purpose talisman against adversity's randomness. And maybe it helps. Maybe meditating and letting go of my anger at people who drive for miles with their left-turn signal flashing would improve the quality of my life, if not its length. Or maybe it would be more the equivalent of forcing a New Yorker to live in rural Maine.

As for the new store down the street from me, it turns out that it sells "yoga-inspired apparel." At first I refused to patronize it, but eventually I broke down. They do free hemming. And that saves me a lot of time—and stress.

Questions for 7.2

1. Explain the relationship between stress and illness that some people claim exists. Why does the author say that this popular mythology both simplifies and generalizes the potential harm of applying it to everything?

2. Why, according to Orenstein, are women today particularly vulnerable to placing the locus of illness in their heads rather than their bodies?

3. What evidence does this article present for the claim that "a positive attitude" was responsible for the 80 percent survival rate of ovarian cancer patients and the similar survival rate of patients with breast cancer?

4. What kind of evidence would add significant support to their claims?

5. What do you make of the Danish study that found that women who were highly stressed were 40 percent *less* likely than others to get breast cancer? Explain your answer.

Is Prayer Good for Your Health?

Stan Cox

As 2007 drew to a close, news media across the country reported on the usual holiday collection of medical miracles—stories that almost always end with patients and family members giving credit to the healing power of prayer.

One survivor, a Christian heavy-metal vocalist who was struck in the neck in December's notorious Colorado church shootings, is now recovering, say his friends and fans, with the aid of prayer vigils throughout the United States and Europe.

And Christmas week, a 46-year-old Beach City, Ohio, surrogate mother, who had originally been thought to be carrying only one fetus, delivered a set of healthy twins after a difficult pregnancy. Her niece, the egg donor, announced that the double birth was the result of prayers she had secretly offered for months.

Selection 7.3

Arising partly out of religious belief and partly out of frustration with high-tech medicine, millions of prayers cross the lips of patients, family members, and even doctors and nurses each day in America's hospitals and examining rooms.

That has prompted a post-2000 wave of research aimed at determining what, if anything, all that praying accomplishes: Can it directly improve patients' health? Does it simply soothe? What happens if the patients aren't told they are being prayed for? And what if they do know—can patients be harmed by prayer? The answers found so far don't seem to be making anyone feel much better.

Say Two Prayers and Call Me in the Morning

A 1998 Harvard Medical School survey estimated that 35 percent of Americans pray for good health and that 69 percent of those who pray find it "very helpful"—a bigger percentage than felt their visits to doctors had been very helpful. A much larger study conducted by the National Institutes of Health in 2002 found 43 percent of people in the United States pray for their own health, and 24 percent seek the prayers of others. Most strikingly, 73 percent of critical-care nurses in a 2005 national survey said they use prayer in their work. Such results are no big surprise. Most Americans are religious believers and can recount for you any number of stories in which prayer ap-

"Is Prayer Good for Your Health," by Stan Cox, from AlterNet, October 2, 2008.

Reprinted with permission by Stan Cox.

peared to heal. The highly respected Sidney Kimmel Comprehensive Cancer Center at Johns Hopkins University has even set up an "intensive prayer unit" to capture whatever benefits it might provide.

For medical prayer to have an effect, no actual divine or supernatural intervention is necessary; belief alone may give a psychological boost to a recovering patient. Any doctor or scientist wishing to lay bare the healing hand of God or the power of "energy medicine" finds that the placebo effect of prayer is much harder to account for than that of pharmaceuticals, which can be dispensed in controlled doses or replaced by sugar pills.

But one type of prayer experiment does attempt to account for the sugar-pill effect and thereby meet the rigorous statistical requirements of scientific journals. In randomized, double-blind studies, the praying is done by people who aren't in contact with the patients, the patients don't know whether they are being prayed for or not (and in some cases don't even know an experiment is going on), and the doctors and researchers don't know who is praying for whom as they go about treating patients and analyzing the data.

It's through such studies that a small cadre of researchers has been trying in recent years to go straight to the source, to determine whether prayers offered from a distance can heal patients' bodies without passing through their minds. Such "distant intercessory prayer" or "distant healing" studies have also become somewhat of a growth industry. Following only three papers published on the subject between 1960 and 1990 and just four during the 1990s, at least 18 new studies have hit the scientific literature since 2000.

Generous federal and private funding has helped fertilize work in this area, but results so far have been underwhelming. The majority of studies show no significant effects, positive or negative. Some actually find prayer harmful. Others have asked more specific questions: whether the benefits of prayer increase with "dosage" (they don't), whether it matters who does the praying (born-again Christians seem to have an edge, says one observer), and even whether prayers can travel back in time (you'll have to wait a bit for the answer to that one).

The Double-Blind Double-Bind

A type of statistical merger—called a "meta-analysis"—of 15 distant-prayer studies, led by researchers at Syracuse University and published in 2006–2007, was unequivocal in concluding that "there is no scientifically discernible effect for distant intercessory prayer on health," regardless of how often or how long patients were prayed for.

In contrast, Dr. David R. Hodge, an assistant professor of social work at Arizona State University, believes he has discerned positive effects of distant prayer on the health of patients. His own 2007 meta-analysis covered 17 papers, most of them in common with those covered in the Syracuse study. He did detect small effects, ones that just scraped past the customarily accepted limit at which they can be considered statistically significant.

That, combined with the fact that six of the 17 papers reported at least some positive effects, led Hodge to suggest that more open-minded medical practitioners might consider using prayer.

Although only small effects have been detected so far (no Bible-caliber tales of patients regaining their sight or rising from the dead in these papers), they're nevertheless important, says Hodge. Whether it's an omnipotent Supreme Being or some as yet unidentified natural force at work, he maintains, the results can be blurred by experimental noise. As he puts it, "If prayer does produce positive outcomes, it is entirely plausible that the effects, as measured by quantitative methods, would be small when assessed in aggregate."

Hodge did take care to run two versions of his meta-analysis, one including and one excluding a controversial 2001 report that distant prayer boosted the success of in vitro fertilization in a Korean fertility clinic. The results, which featured prayed-for women achieving twice the rate of conception as did others, as well as a larger proportion of multiple births, were much more dramatic than others seen in prayer research (and would appear to support the claim of that egg donor in Ohio who prayed for and got twins from her aunt).

The study was soon attacked on several fronts: its allegedly flawed methodology; its renunciation by the original lead author, Dr. Rogerio Lobo of Columbia University; and the conviction on unrelated fraud charges of another author, Daniel Wirth, the person who had organized the Christian prayer groups in the United States that prayed for the Korean women in the study.

But Hodge failed to note the peculiar back-stories of some of the other scientific papers he cited as showing benefits of prayer.

For example, a double-blind 1998 California study found that six months after being prayed for, the health of AIDS patients was significantly better than the health of those who received no prayer. But in 2002, *Wired* magazine reported that while analyzing the data, the study's authors, having failed to find differences in death rates between the two groups, had "unblinded" the data, looked for other health measures that would show a difference and even searched medical records for other health outcomes that had not been part of the original study, all before re-blinding and reanalyzing the data. Statistical results achieved in such a way are considered unreliable at best.

A 2002 study of 39 patients in an intensive-care unit of an unidentified hospital found that those treated with prayer were released from the hospital sooner than patients who weren't; however, the two groups suffered equally from medical complications. The paper appeared in a predominantly non-research publication—the *Journal of Christian Nursing*—alongside articles with titles like "Evelyn and Charles: An Oasis of Love in the ER."

Finally, there was a study published in the *British Medical Journal* purporting to show that prayer can reach backward through time to aid patients' recovery! In 2000, medical professor Leonard Leibovici coded the identities of all bloodstream-infection patients who'd been treated at Rabin Medical Center in Petah-Tikva, Israel, between 1990 and 1996, and ran them through a random-number generator. He then allocated them randomly into two groups, one of which was then prayed for.

Despite having been hospitalized five to 10 years before the experiment was even conceived, the patients in the prayed-for group had, on average, shorter fevers and were discharged more quickly from the hospital.

In subsequent writing, Leibovici made it clear that he hadn't meant the paper to be taken as serious research; rather, it was to stand as a tongue-in-cheek warning that statistical analyses, no matter how valid, cannot be used to draw nonscientific conclusions. But two doctors in Iowa and Texas responded to Leibovici's work in a subsequent issue of the journal, claiming that advanced physics—specifically quantum mechanics—supports the idea of time-traveling prayer.

They even credited Leibovici with what would almost certainly be one of humanity's most amazing achievements, writing that the Israeli professor "may have laid bare a facet of reality—unity and inseparability of all humans across space and time."

However, the odd phenomena associated with quantum physics have never been shown to occur at any scale above the subatomic, let alone among living beings. Dr. Richard Sloan, professor of behavioral medicine at Columbia University and author of the 2006 book *Blind Faith: The Unholy Alliance of Religion and Medicine,* dismisses the invocation of quantum mechanics by prayer advocates as nothing more than "an intellectually cheap way of cowing the listener by appealing to something no one fully understands."

Like Sloan, Dr. Bruce Flamm, a professor of obstetrics and gynecology at the University of California, Irvine, is a prominent critic of medical prayer research. He has been especially harsh in his analysis of the controversial study of in vitro fertilization patients in Korea, saying that the paper exemplifies many of the fallacies inherent in prayer research. He has written in one of his critiques:

> If psychic healers or fortune tellers had claimed to have doubled the success rate of infertility treatments by utilizing tarot cards or Ouija boards, their manuscript would have been immediately rejected as utter nonsense by any legitimate medical journal. Yet, the apparently supernatural results of the Cha/Wirth/Lobo study were accepted and published by a supposedly evidence-based, peer-reviewed medical journal. Why?

Reached by email, Flamm raised another, even more serious argument against prayer in general: "If the creator of the universe actually did respond to intercessory prayer, science would not function. Of course, science does function and quite well." On the other hand, he points out, "if prayer could immediately change the results of a research study, no results of any study on any subject could ever be trusted."

Warning: Prayer May Be Hazardous to Your Health

Harold Koenig, a psychiatrist who directs Duke University's Center for Spirituality, Theology, and Health told the journal *Nature Medicine* in 2005, "Probably saying a 30-second prayer at a key moment has done more good than any psychotherapy or drugs I've prescribed." Whether he was promoting prayer or expressing dissatisfaction with his standard methods, or perhaps both, isn't clear from his statement. But he was clearly assuming that prayer has no negative effects.

That may not be a safe assumption. Consider a 1997 paper examining the possible benefits of prayer for people undergoing treatment for alcohol abuse or dependence. It found that patients who reported that "a family member or friend was already praying for them were found to be drinking significantly more at six months than were those who reported being unaware of anyone praying for them."

What is probably the most widely discussed prayer publication to date—the *Study of the Therapeutic Effects of Intercessory Prayer* (STEP)—also found that prayer may be hazardous to your health. It was conducted by researchers at nine medical institutions, funded by the religious John Templeton Foundation of West Conshohocken, Pa., and published in 2006. The study's results, based on 1,800 patients undergoing coronary bypass surgery, could hardly have been what the researchers had expected.

Among patients who didn't know whether or not they were receiving prayer, the prayed-for and non-prayed-for groups fared the same, so "blind" prayer had no effect. But a third group of patients who were told that they were certain to receive prayer had significantly worse medical outcomes.

Outside observers attributed the negative effects of prayer in the study to phenomena like emotional stress or performance anxiety and suggested that if prayer indeed behaves like a drug that provides no benefits but has potentially harmful side effects, it should not be administered. But the STEP researchers themselves brushed off the one significant finding of their study, writing, "We have no clear explanation for the observed excess of complications in patients who were certain that intercessors would pray for them . . . the excess may be a chance finding."

Richard Sloan scoffs at that explanation: "You can bet that if the results had gone the other way, if prayer had shown a positive effect, they would never have attributed that to chance." Citing the STEP study and others that find pitfalls in prayer, Bruce Flamm warns, "Readers with a scientific world view understand that faith healing does not work but might assume it will at least do no harm. Actually, it can do harm." Some of the broader dangers he points to:

- It can cause patients to shun effective medical care.
- It can lead doctors to diminish their medical efforts.
- It can steer insurers to faith-based interventions.
- It can promote guilt by suggesting that God is somehow punishing a patient with illness or injury and demands penance as the price of recovery.
- It is often linked intimately to prayers for Christian salvation to which a patient might object if informed about it.

Despite what one might expect, Christian evangelicals have no monopoly on remote-prayer research. Much of the work spans several religions or is rooted in New Age spiritualism. The somewhat bafflingly named Monitoring and Actualization of Noetic Trainings (MANTRA) study led by Dr. Mitchell Krucoff of Duke University incorporated distant prayer directed at cardiology patients by Muslim, Jewish, Buddhist and Christian devotees, either with and without in-person "music, imagery and touch therapy."

The study, published in 2005, came to a by now familiar conclusion: "Neither therapy, alone or combined, showed any measurable treatment effect."

While the MANTRA was still in progress, when hopes were still high, journalist Peter Maass followed Krucoff, a cardiologist, through his work day. Before performing an angioplasty on an 80-year-old woman, Krucoff and a nurse practitioner said silent prayers. The prayers were not part of MANTRA, but rather something that the pair did routinely, without patients' knowledge.

This raises the question of whether, having conducted rigorous research showing no statistically detectable benefit of prayer, Krucoff continues to pray for his patients. We can't say for sure—he declined to discuss the MANTRA study with [us]. But in a commentary on the STEP study's headline-making finding of possible harmful side effects from prayer—published the year after his own study—Krucoff and two colleagues wrote that "even well-intentioned intercessory prayer must be scrutinized for safety issues at an equal or even higher level than efficacy measures."

A Cosmic Vending Machine?

Having found apparent benefits of distant prayer in his analyses, David Hodge feels that research on the topic is still in its infancy: "I could see someone making a case for further research on intercessory prayer based upon its wide usage among the general public [and] potential healing effects, and to better understand how it enhances well-being—assuming that it does at all."

But he hastens to add that distant prayer may not be the best investment: "If I had a limited amount of research dollars, I would be inclined to focus my efforts on the results when a client dealing with a psychological or medical challenge prays, meditates, etc."

Alternative therapies are becoming a bigger part of the healthcare industry every year. The National Institutes of Health have received more than $900 million in congressional appropriations since 1999 to study complementary and alternative medical treatments, everything from green tea for skin cancer prevention to expressive-writing therapy for diabetes patients. But the $2.3 million in grants that NIH awarded for research on prayer during that decade has been among the most controversial money it has spent.

Now the flow of taxpayers' money into prayer appears to be slowing or even stopping. No explicitly prayer-related grants have shown up among those funded by NIH's National Center for Complementary and Alternative Medicine since 2004. But private universities and foundations continue to answer grant applicants' prayers, more than compensating for the decrease in federal funding.

"The countless millions of dollars wasted by groups like the Templeton Foundation on superstitious nonsense could have been used to fund legitimate scientific medical research," says Bruce Flamm. "Sadly, they have squandered vast amounts of money that could have been used to study and perhaps cure many diseases."

Pleased with the curtailment of federal prayer funding, Richard Sloan says, "Private foundations are free to fund stupidly if they want. But we should not be recommending interventions that have no explanation in this universe. It's based on a belief that the universe is a cosmic vending machine—a belief that you can deposit prayers in the slot and the desired outcome will appear in the hopper."

And if nothing comes out, those recent studies would suggest, don't try tilting the machine.

Questions for 7.3

1. According to this article, what is "distant healing" and what results do studies of "distant healing" show?
2. How persuasive are these results?
3. Draw up a list of the "evidence" pro and con with respect to the question "Is prayer good for your health?" Which of these studies do you find most and least persuasive and why or why not?
4. What are some of the dangers associated with praying? Assess prayer's negative effects.
5. Why do you think some people are so committed to "proving" that praying for people is a good thing to do?
6. Read this article again, very carefully, and evaluate its conclusions using critical thinking.

It's the Solution, Not the Problem

The last chapter of this book examines some of the explanations of the financial crisis that began in 2008 or earlier in the United States. The enormous meltdown brought with it mortgage foreclosures, job losses, losses of health insurance and retirement funds, and a host of similar calamities. At the time of this writing, the WHAT? was the worst financial crisis in this country had experienced since the Great Depression.

What could explain the collapse of the economy and the extraordinary misery it brought with it? Some people said that the culprit was greed. They maintained that the crisis was caused by people purchasing property—homes, automobiles, household goods—that they could not afford. Greedy people just wanted more. In this way, individuals are held responsible for making irresponsible choices. It is individual behavior that got us into trouble, helped of course by the greed of money managers and financial movers who made millions even as the economy went into a tailspin, bringing down with it the hopes of many Americans.

Other explanations, for example those shared by many conservative thinkers and conservative economic columnists like Kevin A. Hassett of the American Enterprise Institute in the second article in this chapter, point the finger at regulations. In spite of all the evidence to the contrary, neoconservatives continue to maintain that the free market is the best economic system for this country and indeed for the world, and that it is government's attempts to regulate the market that caused the financial crisis.

Jeff Madrick writes in the third article in this chapter that regulation is "the solution, not the problem." He lays out in great detail the failings of the ideology behind the neoliberal economic approach, and he argues for the reregulation of Wall Street and the continued spending of bailout money at an even faster pace in order to create jobs and government projects that will help people survive the crisis and then put in place structural changes in the way our economic system is organized and operates to make sure that a crisis never happens again.

How should a critical thinker evaluate these competing theories and the ideologies on which they are based? These articles offer contrasting views of how the economic system works. Your job is to evaluate how effectively each explains what happened and why. As always, a good place to start is by asking whose interests are served by defining the problems and the solutions in each of these ways.

Further Reading

Ehrenreich, Ben. "Hell No, We Won't Be Foreclosed." *The Nation,* February 9, 2009.

Kotz, David. "Crisis and Neoliberal Capitalism." *Dollars & Sense,* November/December 2008.

Ridgeway, James. "It's the Deregulation, Stupid." Mother Jones, motherjones.com

Wolson, Marty. "Derivatives and Deregulation." *Dollars & Sense,* November/December 2008.

Human Greed Lies at Root of Economic Crisis

Interview with Michael Bolden

Neal Conan

Neal Conan: This is *Talk of the Nation*. I'm Neal Conan in Washington. As Congress, the White House, the Fed and the Treasury Department struggle over the size, shape and nature of the Wall Street bailout, much of the blame game has focused on an unhappy aspect of human nature—greed. The subprime mortgage debacle that poisoned Main Street and then Wall Street, greed. Marauding lenders peddled interest-only mortgages to people who didn't even have to prove they had a job, and corporations never questioned financial

Selection 8.1

instruments they didn't quite understand because they brought in huge profits. But we all blew up this bubble. And now as we face staggering consequences, it's time to ask the nagging little question, could they have done it without us? Were we too keen to flip our houses, sign up for more credit, roll-over our balances . . . ?

Greed and the financial panic, blame it on the lenders and the bankers, but could they have done it without us? . . . We start with Michael Bolden, the copy and production chief at the *Washington Post Magazine,* who wrote a story about getting in a little over his head financially when he bought what he called the house of his dreams. . . .

Conan: Not long after you bought your dream house, you write, it turned into a financial nightmare.

Bolden: Well, we should have seen what was happening at the very beginning. You know, we were hoping to parlay the purchase of this home into wealth. And from the very beginning, we were encountering some financial difficulty. I think that was inspired in part by what was an overwrought and overzealous market. We were counting on using the money that we had from our current house, which we were selling to buy the new property. And we ran into trouble when the person who was buying our home, their loan fell through two days before closing. And that sort of set off a cascade of events that led us down a path that we probably shouldn't have gone down. This

"Human Greed Lies at the Root of Economic Crisis: Interview with Michael Bolden," by Neal Conan, host, *Talk of the Nation,* National Public Radio, September 23, 2008.

Reprinted with permission by Neal Conan.

person couldn't afford to buy our house and so we were like, well, we really want this new house. We're really pursuing this dream. It was a wonderful old house that sort of typified, I think, what a lot of Americans want.

Conan: You described one terrible morning when you go to the closing and you're being asked to sign off on terms for two mortgages that you hadn't seen before that morning, were nothing like what [had] been described to you, and yet you felt—and you guys had bought houses before, this was your fourth house that you'd bought. Nevertheless, with all that experience, you felt tremendous pressure to go ahead and sign.

Bolden: Well, I knew we had been waiting for a month. The people we were buying the house from had graciously sort of agreed to wait on us, but I knew that they were also pursuing a dream. They were retiring and moving from the immediate area. So they weren't going to wait forever. And we had gone to a mortgage broker, told him, you know, a general outline of terms that we wanted. We were counting on being able to get into the house and refinance into a more favorable mortgage. And that day at the closing table, we were faced with a mortgage that had pre-payment penalties, whose interest rate was slightly higher than I think we had banked on. And so the terms were kind of onerous and we were faced with the question, do we sign off on these documents and go ahead, or do we say no and stop the process and risk losing the house? We weren't willing to risk losing the house. And given the availability of easy money at the time, we didn't think it would be a problem refinancing into something more favorable.

Conan: Yet, even though you'd put a lot of work into the house and hoped that a couple of years later you could refinance and get out from under this, well, the storm clouds had gathered by then.

Bolden: Well, the storm clouds had gathered and there was another aspect of the situation that conspired against us. One of the things that happened when the market was overheated was that . . . everybody was so busy—the loan brokers, the appraisers—that they really didn't have time to cross all the T's and dot the I's. When we got ready to refinance, we discovered that the appraiser had actually made a mistake and erroneously put down the square footage of the house as being more than it actually was. So that when someone actually had time to do a considered appraisal, the house was actually valued at less than we thought it would have been at that point. . . . By the time we'd paid for the house, we'd put money into renovations, we actually found ourselves on the losing end.

Conan: So this house that you'd hoped to fix up in a couple of years, make a very fancy bedroom and—you did some of the repairs but not [all], the roof hasn't been fixed and all that stuff, nevertheless you're now still living in it, you'd hoped to have sold it by now and be living in Florida.

Bolden: Well, you know, we were, our previous home, we actually, it doubled in value in four years in the market and so we thought that we could buy this house and it would double in value after we'd put some money into it and that we would be able to sell it for well over a million dollars. We were going to take that profit and probably move to Florida. You know, Americans traditionally have built wealth through their homes and we were no different. That's exactly what we were trying to do. And of course, none of that came to pass as the market collapsed.

Conan: And to some degree you've got to blame, was it greed?

Bolden: Oh, we were definitely greedy. We were motivated by a couple of different things. You know, we already had a lovely home that we could still be living in [to] this day, but this house, the one that we were buying, was somewhat special, it was an older house sitting on two acres of land. And that was a dream that we'd always wanted to pursue. But at the same time, we had seen what could happen if you made the right real estate investment and how your money could double. So we wanted to capitalize on even more of that. And our friends all around us were sort of caught up in the same thing where we had—people in the neighborhood we were living in at the time were all looking to buy that next house and find that next real estate deal that would, you know, get them the most bang for the buck. So, of course now, we all find ourselves in a very different place from where we thought we'd be.

Conan: And a bunch of foreclosure signs up there too, but it was a culture.

Bolden: That's exactly right. If we went to a dinner party or you're just talking with someone across the fence on a Saturday morning, what you'd be talking about was, you know, the unbelievable fortune you'd had to see your property, you know, double in value. That's an extraordinary thing to have happen in only four years worth of time. [The house] that we were living in at the time, we paid 240 for. When we sold that house, you know, we sold it for almost $500,000, and that's just in four years. . . . It is a very lovely home, we are going to continue to stay there. We are going to fix it up gradually and we hope this market recovers.

Conan: Thanks very much. Michael Bolden, copy and production chief of the *Washington Post*. His story about getting in over his head financially appeared in the *Washington Post Magazine* this past Sunday. . . . We're talking about our part and the part that greed played in this particular crisis that we're facing as a country. Let's see if we can get James on the line, James calling us from Lodi in California.

James: [My] basic comment is that there is greed on all parts. And [I] personally, as a home owner, chose to take the easy way out in getting more of the material items by refinancing my home and getting extra stuff that I really shouldn't have gotten or could afford. So . . .

Conan: The material things, that almost sounds spiritual.

[*Laughter*]

James: A little bit. But I mean, it was more of wanting what everybody else had. New car, bigger TV, you know, making your house nicer, you know, getting the refinancing. In my case, I had refinanced with a HELOC. And when I got to the paper signing, they had, instead of doing the original amount that we had agreed upon, they had given me the full estimated value of my home. And so instead of me stopping where I should have stopped, I kept borrowing against it to get this thing or that thing or the other thing, taking, you know, the kids on vacation, whatever have you, instead of being responsible about my money and managing it wisely. I went ahead and made some pretty bad errors. . . .

Conan: . . . Jim Wallis is the founder and president of Sojourners, a Christian evangelical ministry based in Washington, D.C. He wrote a piece for *On Faith* dealing with morality and the economy. He joins us now from the studios of member station KQED in San Francisco. Nice to have you on the program today.

Wallis: Hi, Neal. How are you?

Conan: And there's been a lot of finger pointing at Wall Street and plenty of blame to go around. But the greed was not all on one side, was it?

Wallis: You know, this word greed has really now entered the conversation in a way that I was really startled by. You know, Robert Samuelson, a venerable columnist, said greed and fear, which routinely govern financial markets, have seeded this global crisis. Short-term rewards blinded them to the long-term dangers. I think, Neal, this is both structural and spiritual. And the answers are going to be a combination of social regulation but also self-regulation.

Conan: Greed, famously one of the seven deadly sins but also an aspect of human nature. It's—more—[it's] a familiar emotion.

Questions for 8.1

1. Who or what bears the responsibility for the financial crisis of 2009?
2. In what sense does the moderator of the TV show *Talk of the Nation* hold human beings responsible for the crisis?
3. What evidence does the moderator provide for his attribution of blame?
4. Why does the moderator place the blame there rather than on structural features of the economy?
5. According to this article, what role did the subprime mortgage debacle play in creating the crisis?
6. According to this article, what role did the money lenders who encouraged people to buy properties that they could not afford play in creating the crisis?
7. According to Michael Bolden, what role did the overzealous market play in creating this problem?
8. What protections existed that could slow the purchase process down so that a buyer could adequately evaluate the situation and decide whether to go ahead with the purchase?
9. How did the Holder family expect to increase its wealth?
10. Was this a reasonable expectation? Explain your answer.
11. Based on your reading of this article, do you think that human greed is at the root of the economic crisis? Do you agree or disagree? Explain your answer.

The Lesson from the [Fiscal] Crisis: Regulations Are Worthless

Kevin A. Hassett

When people trust that the government will protect them and it fails to, disaster strikes. But failure is what government is best at. Protect yourself.

Is free-market capitalism to blame for today's economic crisis? Despite well-documented empirical evidence of the relationship between economic freedom and growth, many believe unrestrained capitalism is the cause of recent turmoil in the global economy. A more accurate story, however, is that excessive government regulation, not free-market capitalism, is responsible for aggravating the current economic contraction.

> **Selection 8.2**

If we gathered together a random sample of the world's citizens a year ago, and asked them to characterize the core principles of a successful society, then "free market capitalism" would surely have received nearly unanimous support. A country should, the consensus was, strive to place its wealth in private hands, and allow private individuals to transact among themselves with as little influence from government as possible. Such an organization would, the story went, provide the maximum welfare to a nation's citizens.

One could hardly blame individuals for responding in that way. Over the past twenty years, capitalism spread to every corner of the globe, even to former communist nations such as China and Russia. With it came prosperity. Moreover, the countries that bet the most on capitalism, like the United States, radically outperformed nations that hedged their bets and erected elaborate government constraints on free markets.

The previous consensus emerged because of the personal experience of billions of citizens that has been widely documented in a large empirical literature. There has been a striking positive relationship between economic freedom and economic growth. A 2000 report by Harvard University economist Robert Barro found that property rights and free markets were the most important institutional elements for promoting economic growth. Similarly, the Fraser Institute's annual *Economic Freedom of the World Report* has documented numerous times that the free-market recipe of competition,

"The Lesson from the [Fiscal] Crisis: Regulations Are Worthless," by Kevin A. Hassett, American Enterprise Institute for Public Policy Research, January 28, 2009.

entrepreneurship and investment activity is crucial for fostering long-term economic growth.

The case seemed closed. Yet today, if one were to gather the same individuals, their answers would be fundamentally different. The global economy is in free fall, and some of the most "free," like Iceland, have been hit the hardest.

We are at a turning point where the world's citizens are fundamentally reassessing their commitment to capitalism.

When projecting where the debate will end up, it is important to note at the outset that this is not the first time that we have reached this crossroads.

The idea that free market capitalism is the best organizing principle for a civilization is an old one, dating back at least to Adam Smith's *Wealth of Nations*, which was published in 1776. The idea that capitalism has shortcomings is just as old as capitalism itself. Critics from the early Mercantilists to Marx and Keynes have exposed capitalism's weaknesses, and offered alternatives.

No creation of man, even capitalism, is perfect and immune to revision. History fluctuates. When times are good, men take great satisfaction in their creations, perhaps giving themselves too much credit for their good fortune. And when times are bad, there is a tendency to look back to the academy and give new authority to critics that warned that our creations were always bound to fail.

The history of capitalism is one of ebbs and flows. When capitalist economies boom, its critics are quiet, or at least ignored. But when capitalist economies experience collapse, as is sadly the case today, then introspection and criticism can even lead to revolution.

But throughout the trials, capitalism survived because it significantly outperformed any alternative. Revolutions have the most force when a sufficient mass of revolutionaries becomes convinced that some alternative structure is superior. In the current episode, the case for a radical reduction in our commitment to freedom and private action would require evidence that the current crisis was caused by excessive freedom, but also, and more crucially, evidence that something else works better.

It seems enormously unlikely that that such evidence will be found.

In terms of the causes of the crisis, financial market historians will certainly cite the U.S. real estate market as the spark that ignited the conflagration. But the distinguishing characteristic of that market is not wild-eyed freedom, but rather, excessive government intervention.

This is clearly demonstrated by the recent catastrophic failures of Fannie Mae and Freddie Mac, which precipitated the wide-spread instability in the financial markets. In 1992, the government-sponsored enterprises were given the mission of expanding "affordable housing." In order to fulfill strict regulations imposed by the Department of Housing and Urban Development (HUD), Fannie and Freddie purchased and guaranteed large numbers of subprime and other nontraditional loans and eventually became the primary customers of AAA-rated subprime-mortgage pools.

Although the enormous risk created within the financial system did not go unnoticed, there was little political will at the time to eliminate the hazard. Indeed, one of the world's most famous capitalists saw the dangers very early on. In 2005, Alan Greenspan warned that if Fannie and Freddie "continue to grow, continue to have the low capital that they have, continue to engage in the dynamic hedging of their portfolios, which they need to do for interest rate risk aversion, they potentially create ever-growing potential systemic risk down the road." Further, Greenspan asserted, "we are placing the total financial system of the future at a substantial risk."

In 2005, legislation was proposed which would have reformed the entities and eliminated their investments in risky assets. The legislation failed, however, because of the obstruction of Democrats such as Christopher Dodd and Barney Frank, who received massive political contributions from Fannie and Freddie.

If markets had been left to themselves, then the dodgy loans that brought down our financial system would never have been made.

This leaves open the question why the toxic assets spread so rapidly to the willing buyers throughout the world. The simplest explanation is that the poison received the U.S. government's seal of approval, and too many trusted that seal.

The next piece of evidence that an opponent of free market capitalism would have to deliver in order to win new adherents is documentation that countries that were more skeptical of capitalism, and fettered it accordingly, were able to avoid the crisis, or at least suffered less than the capitalist swashbucklers.

Recent data on economic performance across countries suggests the opposite. Although no country has escaped recent economic turmoil unscathed, an international comparison of stock market performances over the last year that I recently published in the *National Review* shows that countries that were economically free (like Canada), while still suffering downturns, have fared much better on average than more regulated economies (like the Netherlands).

There is no model one can point to that worked. No regulator on earth was ahead of the curve on this crisis.

Indeed, if we have learned anything it is that regulation was worthless. Like the failed communist planners before them, government regulators were fundamentally unable to deliver on their promises. So why should we expect them to do better next time?

Regulators likely failed because, as was long ago argued by University of Chicago economist George Stigler, they become captives of the firms they were supposed to regulate.

Having corrupt police is worse than having no police at all. When people trust that the government will protect them and it fails to, disaster strikes. But failure is what government is best at. Protect yourself.

All of which makes it hard to see how the current crisis could go down in history as providing evidence of the inadequacy of capitalism. A corrupt government body doled out an excessive amount of loans, building a house of cards that eventually collapsed catastrophically. When the collapse came, no amount of regulation provided immunity to the repercussions. Those who put the most faith in government suffered the worst.

In the end, those with the brightest future will leave this crisis where they began it: committed capitalists.

Questions for 8.2

1. What lesson does the author, Kevin Hassett, say he learned from this crisis of 2008–2009?

2. Give three examples of the kinds of regulations the author is talking about.

3. Explain how or why free market capitalism is or is not to blame for the 2009 economic crisis.

4. What, according to Hassett, has been the relationship between economic freedom and economic growth?

5. The author maintains that capitalism has survived because it significantly outperformed any alternative. What evidence does he provide to support this claim?

6. Has the wealth gap stayed the same, increased, or declined during the past twenty years? What do the income gap and the wealth gap tell us about how our economy is structured?

7. Which groups in U.S. society have benefited from the way opportunity and wealth have been distributed and which groups have seen their assets and their opportunities decline?

8. According to Hassett, what role did the U.S. government play in the collapse of the economy?

9. In light of all the evidence that suggests that capitalism is not the solution to the problem of our economy, explain why Hassett continues to defend the capitalist system. Does he make his case?

It's the Solution, Not the Problem

Jeff Madrick

Faith-based claims about the dangers of big government do not stand up to the evidence.

The financial crisis jeopardizing living standards around the world is the direct result of the antigovernment attitudes that began to spread in the United States as far back as the 1970s and reached their height in the George W. Bush administration. It had become conventional wisdom that high levels of taxes, government spending and regulation—in sum, big government—inevitably undermine a nation's prosperity. The claims, embraced enthusiastically by business, apparently also struck a deep intuitive chord among Americans. The dangers of big government had become so obvious to so many over the past

Selection 8.3

thirty years that they hardly seemed to require demonstration any longer, even among many Democrats. Government was widely seen as the problem and rarely the solution, a sharp reversal of attitudes that prevailed for the first two-thirds of that century. Cutting taxes was the main rallying cry, but deregulation was its close cousin. Starting in the 1980s, with Ronald Reagan's presidency in particular but extended by George H. W. Bush, Bill Clinton and George W. Bush—as well as Alan Greenspan, the ideological Federal Reserve chair who won far more credibility than he deserved—the government reduced its regulatory oversight radically over the course of a generation.

President Clinton proudly announced the new position in 1996. "The era of big government is over," he said with fanfare in his State of the Union address, the year of his presidential re-election bid. He successfully raised taxes on better-off Americans in 1993 but with the express purpose of reducing the federal deficit, not developing new social programs. In the ensuing years, considerable regulatory damage was done. Even after severe financial storms in the late 1990s in Asia and Russia and at hedge funds in New York, neither the Republicans nor the Democrats asked for new regulatory authority or requirements for disclosure of more information. Now even Greenspan acknowledges serious errors of judgment. No one knows the extent of the liabilities of financial firms today because of the lack of federal oversight of

"It's the Solution, Not the Problem: Faith-Based Claims about the Dangers of Big Government Do Not Stand Up to Evidence," by Jeff Madrick, from *The Nation,* November 24, 2008. Reprinted with permission from the November 24, 2008, issue of *The Nation.* For subscription information, call 1-800-333-8536. Portions of each week's *Nation* magazine can be accessed at http://www.thenation.com.

financial derivatives. The Clinton administration signed off on the end of the Glass-Steagall legislation, which had separated in law and spirit commercial and investment banking, and Clinton's Treasury secretary prevented the Commodities Futures Trading Commission from actively regulating derivatives.

But it was the George W. Bush administration that took up the Reagan banner with energy and vindictive delight. Bush engineered enormous tax cuts, but the loosening of regulations was also integral to his philosophy. In 2004, for example, the Securities and Exchange Commission undid restrictions on how much investment banks could borrow, even as they made enormous profits. In return, the banks volunteered to open their books to the SEC, though this option was never aggressively pursued. Bush's appointee as SEC chair, Christopher Cox, formerly a conservative Congressman, enforced the program with the deliberate Bush-style laxity that has characterized the administration's management of the Food and Drug Administration, the Environmental Protection Agency, the Federal Aviation Administration and, of course, the Federal Emergency Management Agency, which so tragically mangled the Hurricane Katrina rescue efforts. Cox has admitted that the voluntary program did not work and has urged comprehensive securities regulation at last.

All of this is part of a mythology about the dangerous consequences of big government that does not and never did stand up to economic evidence. According to the best mainstream economic research, big-government and high-tax nations simply do not grow any more slowly than nations with proportionally lower levels of government spending and taxes. They do not have lower levels of productivity. The lack of any statistical relationship between taxes and economic prosperity suggests government must often be doing something right.

After all, the fastest growth of social programs in history—the rise of the so-called welfare state—took place in the rich Western nations and Japan over the three decades after 1950. Over that same period, which included the sharp rise in oil prices in the 1970s, the economies of these same countries experienced rapid growth. Today, no government of a Western nation spends less than 10 percent of gross domestic product (GDP), and many spend much more, on its poor, unhealthy and aged—what economists call social transfers—and all are immensely wealthy by historical standards. In addition to spending on social transfers, they also spend significantly on education and infrastructure, and they all remain vibrant democracies as well.

Because most of these high-tax economies do well, much of that tax money evidently must be spent constructively, on programs that inspire a sense of confidence and promote good health, education and efficient transportation. There may well be moderate disincentives to invest and work, but many of the programs are intelligently oriented to minimize these. For example, even high levels of unemployment insurance, a particular bête noire of conservatives, can remove less productive workers from the labor force and minimize any damaging consequences from shirking work.

Intelligent regulations, in turn, enable markets to work better by making information more available and reducing abuse and corruption. Regulations can save a lot of money over time, even if they cost more in the short run, as the current experience painfully shows. The evidence does not deter opponents of government. Many critics argued, for example, that Sweden's welfare state had gone too far in the 1980s—taxes were too high and wages too generous. Incomes compared with those of the rest of the wealthy countries were no longer near the top of the tables. Adjustments were made in Sweden, including tax cuts, and conditions improved. But Sweden did not cut taxes or social spending nearly to U.S. levels, or even to those of Britain. To the contrary, social transfers remained a very high proportion of national income, roughly 30 percent of GDP, not including education expenditures. The United States expends only about 13 percent of GDP on such social transfers (Social Security, Medicare, unemployment insurance, housing and poverty).

Yet with such high levels of social transfers, the growth rate of GDP per person in Sweden from the mid-1990s was as high through the mid-2000s as the growth rate of the United States or most European nations—many of which equaled America's GDP growth rate per capita during this period (which included the Clinton boom years).

The average compensation for manufacturing workers in Sweden is about equal to that of America. (To make the wages comparable in this example, they are adjusted for what is called purchasing power parity—the amount of goods and services the wage actually buys.) Sweden's productivity, which many economists argue is inevitably damaged by high levels of social transfers, has not fallen off the table. It is about 87 percent of America's level. Although America's productivity is 15 percent higher than the average of nations in the Organization for Economic Co-operation and Development (OECD)—the two dozen or so richest nations in the world—it is lower than or at best equal to that of a half-dozen nations with much higher taxes and rates of social spending. Roughly half the OECD countries pay higher or equivalent wages to workers in manufacturing, and almost all provide more benefits than do U.S. companies.

Let us now look at how the changing size of American government has affected U.S. prosperity in recent years. In a 2002 foreword to a new edition of his popular 1962 book *Capitalism and Freedom,* Milton Friedman wrote that America had at last recognized the damage done by big government. He apparently had the Clinton boom of the late 1990s in mind. But during the Clinton boom, which Friedman implied had to do with less government, tax receipts rose to 20 percent of GDP, much higher than at any time since the final years of World War II. Federal spending—though it grew more slowly under Clinton, largely because of the peace dividend following the cold war and the slower growth of healthcare costs—remained at higher levels than those in the early 1970s, when Friedman was arguing that government was much too big and was bound to stimulate inflation. In the early 1970s, at that level of government spending, inflation was rising rapidly; in the late 1990s, it was falling.

Some still argue, of course, that the 1981 income tax cuts under Reagan produced the Clinton boom. Given that they occurred fifteen years earlier, the claim is farfetched on the face of it. Reagan did not even cut taxes overall. While income taxes were cut, which conservative economists argue should have provided wonderful incentives for economic growth, payroll taxes for Social Security and Medicare were markedly increased. Total taxes as a proportion of GDP were about the same in Reagan's last year in office as they were in three of the four years of Jimmy Carter's presidency.

What Reagan did was undermine the impact of regulations, largely failing to enforce or implement many of them. Despite the lower income tax rate and persistent deregulation, productivity growth rates (adjusted for the ups and downs of the business cycle) did not improve under Reagan or his successor, George H. W. Bush. The productivity takeoff began in 1996, not long after the Clinton income tax increase. Harvard economist Martin Feldstein, Republican House leader Dick Armey and others predicted that the tax increase would have the opposite effect.

How did the wealthiest nation in history come to believe for a generation, even when it was prosperous in the late 1990s, that it was not wealthy enough to provide what was needed in a more complex and global society?

In the past, when America required canals, railroads and highways, it financed them. When it needed better and broader education, it provided it. When it needed sewer and sanitation systems, and vaccines to prevent widespread disease, it created them. When unemployment became a fact of industrial life, it insured workers against it. When America was at its best, it did not look back and say, We never did this before so we can't do it now. Ultimately it did what was necessary.

Part of the nation's new agenda must be to rid itself of the deep-seated pessimism that it does not acknowledge. Promising a new "morning in America," Reagan ironically ushered in the age of limits he accused Carter of creating. With Reagan, slow wage growth and high levels of unemployment became accepted. Today's coming deep recession is a consequence.

America has no free and high-quality daycare or pre-K institutions to nourish and comfort two-worker families, and work and family are undermined as a consequence. College has become far more expensive, and attendance is bifurcated by class: the privileged go to the best colleges, and good jobs are increasingly available only to those who attend the best colleges. Transportation infrastructure has been notoriously neglected. It is decaying and has not been adequately modernized to meet energy-efficient standards or global competition. America has not responded to a new world of high energy costs and global warming. The country has a healthcare system that is out of control, providing inadequate quality at very high prices—specializing in high-technology medicine at the expense of better overall care. And its financial system has run amok. Speculation and financial panic reminiscent of the harsh 1800s has been the result. Most important, average incomes have been flat or only slightly higher for a generation; for men, that has been true since the early 1970s. In the 2000s, compensation for men and women has fallen. As we enter a recession, wages are about to fall sharply.

These facts amount to about as conclusive a proof as history ever provides that the ideology applied in this generation has failed. This was Reagan's Trojan horse, disguised as optimism. He sent in a plan to reduce help to most Americans under the guise of an ideology of personal responsibility that would ultimately make everyone better off; instead it largely helped an increasingly privileged upper tier. From the economic evidence, history and the performance of other nations, we know the following: if federal, state and local governments absorb another 4 or 5 percent of GDP in America, it will not inhibit growth or undermine entrepreneurial spirit, productivity or prosperity if the spending is well channeled. Government absorbs much more of national income in other nations whose prosperity is the equivalent of or perhaps superior to America's. If government programs are managed well, they will enhance productivity. A rise in government spending of 5 percent of GDP will raise approximately $750 billion a year for federal, state and local governments to provide protection to workers, finance social programs, maintain an adequate regulatory presence and significantly raise the level of investment in transportation, energy, education and healthcare. Once we emerge from this recession—and only after that—part and perhaps all of this $750 billion can be paid for with higher taxes.

Let's try to keep the discussion more politically practical, however. If we lower our sights to an additional 3 percent of GDP for new government programs, the nation would have more than $450 billion a year with which to work. Four hundred fifty billion dollars a year could make Social Security entirely solvent by current estimates, with no further reductions in benefits; provide universal pre-K education to America's 3- to 5-year-olds; and leave enough money to pay two years of tuition for all college students. Thirty billion dollars a year could go a long way toward repairing and updating transportation infrastructure and making it far more energy efficient. Some competent scientists argue that we could transfer the nation from fossil fuel to solar energy for only a little more than that a year.

What seems to many Americans like pragmatic limitations on spending, the proper role of government [and] responsible fiscal management will very likely someday be seen for what they truly are: a reflection of deep pessimism, the rise in power of vested interests seeking tax cuts and special benefits, and a tragic forgoing of responsibility. Boldness of government does not mean that the right choices will always be made. The Iraq War serves as a supreme and tragic reminder of government activism gone awry. But liberals make errors too, and once a government program has started, it is indeed hard to close down.

This should not be a deterrence. We tolerate wrong choices and a lot of waste in business in order not to suppress its "animal spirits." And it is hard to shut down businesses as well. Consider the multiple bailouts on Wall Street right now, and also the recent loans to automakers. But the government has been bailing out financial and other firms for many years: Chrysler in the 1970s, Continental Illinois and the savings and loan associations in the 1980s, the creditors of Long-Term Capital Management in the 1990s and so on. Such examples understate the breadth of government bailouts. When the Federal Reserve rapidly loosened monetary policies in 1972, 1987, 1998 and 2001, it did so to bail out the excesses of business as well.

With an annual GDP of $15 trillion, the United States has the resources and capabilities to recapture its energies and optimism. Government can and must be a full partner to business in economic development and a senior partner in the equitable distribution of benefits and true practical freedoms. What history and contemporary examples teach us is that the nation has the capacity to regulate, tax and invest adequately in public goods without undermining the entrepreneurial capacity and material prosperity of the nation.

Granted, attitudes have momentarily turned in favor of financial regulation and government bailouts. But is the attitudinal conversion merely skin-deep? Not only must the nation stem the draining of capital from the financial system; it must also stimulate the economy to raise it from steep and painful recession. Solving the financial crisis will not be enough, and deepening recession will lead to more financial emergencies as homeowners default on more mortgages and even businesses start to default on their debt.

The re-regulation of Wall Street will be a pressing challenge to the newly elected President Obama. But the main challenge will be to provide the stimulus the economy needs to avoid tragedy while investing in America's health-care, education, broadband, green-energy technology and transportation—the assets it needs to compete in a more competitive world. We shall see whether we will renounce the bad habit of ideology in favor of the pragmatism America always exhibits in its best moments.

Questions for 8.3

1. What, according to Madrick, is "the problem"?
2. How does he explain the origins and nature of the current financial crisis?
3. What policies and practices of the Bush administration does the author specifically identify as part of the problem?
4. Does the author believe that economic evidence is available to support the conservatives' claim that big government is the cause of the crisis?
5. What does Madrick mean by "intelligent regulations" and how does he explain this approach?
6. What specific results of the deep recession we experienced does he point to as its consequences?
7. What would the results be if we allocated an additional 3 percent of GDP for new government programs? What could the $450 billion a year make possible?
8. Madrick argues that the challenge we face is to provide the stimulus the economy needs to deal with the crisis while investing in healthcare, education, transportation, and green energy technology that will allow us to compete in a more competitive world. Has he persuaded you that this will be possible?
9. What would it mean to think outside the box?

CONCLUSION

What's the Problem?
Questions and Answers

Thinking is a tricky business. Learning to think *critically* is even trickier. That's because critical thinking is as much about getting the *questions* right as it is about coming up with the right answers. If the problem is predicated on the wrong question or adopts the wrong conceptual framework, trying to answer it will lead you down the wrong path, possibly depositing you at a dead end or, even worse, getting you stuck in the mud.

1. Select two or three articles in this book that you think best exemplify critical thinking and then explain why you chose them.
2. What about the way the articles pose the problem(s) makes you think they are good examples?
3. Which set of article-concluding questions was most helpful in helping you analyze what it means to think critically?
4. Look at the articles again and select the two articles that you think provide the worst examples of critical thinking and then go on to explain why.
5. What are some other problems or questions that provide good examples of what critical thinking involves?

Acknowledgments

Many thanks to the friends and colleagues who contributed to *What's the Problem?*, including Steve Shalom, Naomi Miller, Joan Dornhoefer, Elizabeth Minich, Beverly Guy-Sheftall, Barbara Corado Pope, Lois Tigay, and the many others whose names should be here but aren't. Mea culpa.

And my sincere thanks to my terrific editor, Erik Gilg, who is always supportive and always willing to think outside the box with me, and to the staff at Worth Publishers, which does such a stellar job for each new book. To that end, thanks to Elizabeth Widdicombe, President; Catherine Woods, Senior Publisher; Jaclyn Castaldo, Assistant Editor; Tracey Kuehn, Associate Managing Editor; Dana Kasowitz, Project Editor; Penny Hull, Copy Editor; Babs Reingold, Art Director; Kevin Kall, Designer; and Katrina Washington, who cleared permissions for this book.

And of course to my partner, Greg Mantsios, and our children Alexi Mantsios and Andrea Mantsios, as we strive together to be the best of critical thinkers in this challenging world.

Index

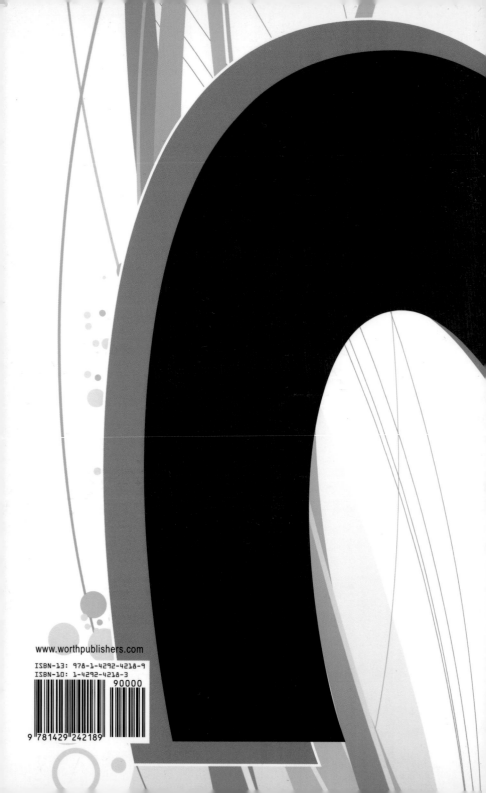

www.worthpublishers.com

ISBN-13: 978-1-4292-4218-9
ISBN-10: 1-4292-4218-3

90000

9 781429 242189